CAN BLACK PEOPLE GROW HAIR?

And other questions that bridge the racial gap
between understanding and being understood.

Andrea Krystal

MANIFOLD GRACE
Publishing House LLC

Can Black People Grow Hair? And other questions that bridge the racial gap between understanding and being understood. Copyright © 2021, Andrea Krystal

Cover Design: Ashley Santoro
Photog: Kaitlyn Bowman

Ref: Brené Brown: *Daring Greatly: How the Courage to Be Vulnerable Transforms the Way We Live, Love, Parent, and Lead; 9781592408412:* Avery An imprint of Penguin Random House; designed by Spring Hoteling

ISBN: 978-1-952926-05-1
ISBN: 978-1-952926-10-5 (ebook)

Printed in the United States of America

Published by Manifold Grace Publishing House, LLC
www.manifoldgracepublishinghouse.com
Southfield, Michigan 48033

Dedication

To all those in the past, present, and future who caught a glimpse of the human capacity for equality, and decided it was worth risking everything to achieve.

Thank you.

Table of Contents

Introduction

I know what it's like being the only Black person in a crowd and having everyone treat you as if you speak for the entire Black community. I know that overwhelming feeling of being surrounded by people who are looking to you to provide their Black experience. I understand how frustrating it can feel when people make comments, or ask questions that seem to lump you into a general category, when you know you are your own person - independent from anyone else. It's frustrating, exhausting, and sometimes down right annoying. And what's more is, you feel this pressure to keep a smile on your face and play the role of the jolly Black woman or man. No one wants to run the risk of your annoyance showing and being labeled as another angry Black person. Y'all, I know the struggle. I feel you. I hear you. I've been you.

There is also another character in this story that needs to be considered, that character is the one asking the questions. The person who doesn't know what they don't know. Now, I'm well aware that the idea of someone not having an awareness of Black life, or hardships, is a hard pill to swallow for some. Because, well, Google and it's 2021. Trust me when I say that more often than not, I get some kind of rebuttal from those in the Black community when I express empathy towards any kind of ignorance. And it usually comes in the form of an eyeroll or heavy sigh. I would be lying if I said I didn't second some of those feelings.

Yes, we all would like to believe that adults are empowered enough to utilize all of the many educational tools at their disposal today. Yes, we would like to believe that people wouldn't place the burden on someone else to provide them with all of their Black education. Yes, we would hope that people would take some kind of personal responsibility for where they are in the development of their world view, but as most of us know, this is not always the case. I think we can all agree that you will never have to look far to find various forms of ignorance about various subjects. The reality is that what seems like common sense to some, isn't all that common to others.

Are you the person who usually feels out of their element around Black people? Maybe if you're honest with yourself, you might feel a mix of curiosity and discomfort when they're around? If so, you are not alone. You're not the only one struggling to make sense of things, or are overwhelmed with the inner work it would take to challenge your own biases. The truth is, we all have some kind of bias about something. The difference is that biases such as what color socks you prefer, are not the same as the bias of believing that certain people groups are better employees than Black people. One is a bias based on personal preference, while the other is a bias based in judgement. While no sock will ever be harmed by your preference, people are harmed in all kinds of ways by the biases that go unchecked in our lives.

As Black people we recognize the face of implicit bias

because it's been staring at us our whole lives. It's true that so many of us in the Black community feel the weight of being generalized, picked apart, and treated as if we're a living, breathing Blacktionary. We are people. We are more than just an outlet for curious minds. We are often teetering between trying to be ourselves, fully and uniquely, and also shouldering the fact that we may be someone's only Black experience. I'd like to invite my community to ask ourselves if we're doing a similar thing to the people that we are frustrated with?

Stay with me a moment and think about it. Is there ever a time, when based on their actions, we draw multiple conclusions about "all of them", not taking into account everyone's individuality? We come to a conclusion that they are all ignorant. That they don't know anything about us. They'll never understand us. That they're insensitive, irreverent, have an agenda, or they will use whatever we say and twist it to align with whatever preconceived notions they already have. We base our conclusions off of a multitude of things like interactions we've had, assumptions we've made, stories we've heard, and what our parents have taught us. Since I don't know your story, I'm not going to tell you that you're wrong. I'm also not going to tell you that you're right. The reality is, there are all kinds of reasons and motives behind why people do what they do. Whether it's us asking the questions or making assumptions, or it's someone else doing it to us, the thing I want every person who's reading this book to consider is the ease with which we judge everyone else by their actions, and yet we often want people to judge us by our intentions.

We judge others based on what they do and we judge ourselves by what we mean. I don't think I have to point out the double standard here and if you're honest with yourself, I think it's easily recognizable. So, with that said, I want you, yes you, to ask yourself a couple of questions; and I mean actually ask yourself. If I have the ability to do something that may come off as insensitive to someone else, when I actually mean well, is it possible that there are people who come off as insensitive to me and yet actually mean well? Is it possible that I am not the only person who struggles to sometimes have their actions and intentions align?

My friend, these are some ego crushing questions I'm prompting you to ask yourself, so if you feel a little uncomfortable - GOOD! Get comfortable with feeling uncomfortable! It isn't until we allow space for challenging our comfort zones and questioning why we do what we do, that we will be able to make progress in closing the racial divide. It's not until we do this deep work that we can close the gap on the many forms of discrimination and division being played out in our world today. I think it's safe to say that it's easy for us to get stuck in the habit of humanizing ourselves when we need grace, but leaving very little grace for others because often, if we're honest, we tend to have pretty high opinions of ourselves on either side and when our ego is calling the shots, it also blocks our view. Ego cemented by tradition can blind us to ourselves. The narratives we've created that say "I've been this way for 50 years now and I've been doing just fine. I don't see any reason to change", the "Well I'm only human", and the infamous "That's just how I was raised" will have you believing that the only way to interact with the world around you is the way you know. These limiting beliefs inhibit us from being able to see past ourselves and our own experiences. So, as you can see this is some deep work we're talking about here. This isn't as simple as "everyone just needs to get along". The healing of this divide of communities involves the reworking and possibly undoing of frameworks that have been fortified by generations of belief.

My heart's purpose for this book is to invite communities to explore how the "Us vs Them" mentality is literally eating away at the fibers of humanity. Each and every human has the capacity for hate and all that accompanies it. Within all of us lies the duality of beauty and ugliness. If we wanted to, we could choose to override our internal checks and balances and let whatever naturally arises be played out in our lives. We'd find out that all the things we shamed other people for being capable of, we in fact are capable of too. At the end of the day, it's our choices that dictate how we show up in the world. It's our choice to put in the work of dismantling systemic injustice. It's our choice not to shy away from tough conversations. It's our choice to be honest with ourselves about ourselves. It's our choice to purposefully engage with those different from us, and it's our choice to take those same differences and turn them into celebrations instead of weapons that we use against each other. Together we are a beautiful tapestry of color, pattern, and texture! Yet each time we indulge our choice to hate, murder, and suppress someone because of their distinctives, we cause rips and snags that become our undoing.

When we choose to deny other people's truths because

we don't want to take an honest look at our own, we are adding to, not taking away from, racism's power. When we choose to let our frustration shame people for where they are in their awareness journey, we are helping to perpetuate a cycle of fear and misunderstanding which inevitably feeds into division. This isn't about needing to agree with everyone and this isn't about not challenging others to be accountable for themselves. This is about humanity coming to a place in which we feel more of a sense of duty to the way in which each other thrives or declines.

My hope is to challenge assumptions on what people's intentions are, while also giving an invitation to move from intention to action. My mission is to help us all seek understanding of intentions, look frankly at our actions, and engage in a deep-dive conversation of the "Why" with empathy, honesty, and vulnerability. We have to move beyond ourselves, our egos, our assumptions, and our traditions. We have to shed light wherever we can if we are going to be a part of healing the emotional, psychological, and spiritual wounds racism has created within people of all colors and communities. We've got to do better and it starts within, not with "them".

ONE - Can Black People Grow Hair?

Yes, this was an actual question I was asked years ago by a white girlfriend of mine. I can't remember all of the circumstances surrounding the how, what, when, and where of the question, but I do remember vividly the crossroads I felt myself come to the moment she asked me. In a matter of seconds, I felt like I had split personalities that were duking it out! Like that visual of the little devil on one shoulder and an angel on the other shoulder, I had something similar going on but it was a lil sista on one shoulder that had the attitude of Lisa Landry in Sister Sister saying "Now what's THAT supposed to mean?!" And on the other shoulder was an old Black Baptist woman telling me to "Walk in the spirit, baby. Walk in the spirit".

Don't think for a moment that just because I've written this book proposing that we be more receptive to people's curiosity that it means I don't get tempted to step outside myself and recite a more direct version of what I'm thinking because I DO! This friend even asked me the question in the most sweet and matter-of-fact-way and I was still tempted to

1

be passive aggressive in my answer and be like "Can YOU grow hair? Of course, Black people can grow hair, what kind of question is that?!" However, I knew there wasn't some negative intent behind her inquiry, but then again, I knew her. I knew her character and her heart before I observed her actions, so I felt confident in the intent. I'm not so naive, however. I know this isn't always the case. Sometimes you're going to encounter a complete stranger who inspires these make-you-wanna-say-hmm moments, and you won't have anything to go on when it comes to being able to feel out their intention or motive. You just have to try to be discerning of the moment and then decide what takes precedence to you in that moment: what you're feeling or what you're not understanding.

So, after I had my split personality moment and was able to look at my friend for who they were, and who they had been to me, my heart began to soften and I recognized the precious opportunity I was presented with, to be able to build a bridge of understanding where there currently wasn't any. I was presented with a need that I knew I could fill and in doing so, one less misconception would be floating about in the world. I kept my answer rather simple, but informative enough. I said "Yep, Black people can grow hair. Just like in the white community or any other people group there are a variety of hair types. Some thick, some thin, some grow very quickly while others take a lot of care to inspire growth, and some struggle to have healthy hair. It's the same for the Black community as every other community." You want to know what her response was? She said matter of factly, "Oh. Yea, that makes sense though I wasn't sure" and then casually went

2

back to whatever our conversation was prior to the question. It wasn't an awkward or exhausting exchange, though I would be lying if I said that it didn't have the potential to be! I've been involved in "conversations" with people who have asked questions like these but who weren't asking with the goal of gaining understanding. They were asking to antagonize and to stir the pot. They were hoping to engage in an argument that would help fuel their belief that Black people are too sensitive, too serious, and always angry. Well, if this had been one of those kinds of conversations, I would have had to respond with a resounding "I am not the one, girlfriend!". When I was younger and felt like I always needed to prove myself, I would often go toe-to-toe with these folks, but not anymore. I've learned over the years that there is no having a mutually engaging discussion with someone who is trying to bait you. You'll just end up walking right into a trap no matter what angle you try to come at the conversation with.

The reality is that every interaction with another human has the potential for hostility, especially if there's already so many differences that people can draw attention to. However, I'm sharing this exchange with you to give an example of how, even when a question may seem like common sense to you, there is a choice you are presented with to allow your response to be inspired by pure emotion or empathy. The inspiration you choose to let guide your response will ultimately play a large role in either building a bridge of understanding that will empower someone else with the ability to stop the cycle of misinformation, or it will discourage them from ever wanting to seek out the knowledge they lack again and as a result will only further cement whatever misinformation they currently have. Whatever they know, whether correct or not, will be what they share with others. So how we respond is so important and is so much bigger than any initial offense or irritation we may experience.

Now I know that if you're Black the idea of being someone's Black spirit guide sounds exhausting because I'm sure that like me, many of you have already been doing this your whole life. Luckily, that is not at all what I'm proposing. This is not about going around and feeling like you have some duty to educate everyone you meet who doesn't have a broad worldview because trying to do this would literally be a full-time job! This isn't about placing the entire burden of someone else's Black experience on your shoulders. This isn't even about going into long in-depth explanations when people ask questions so that they walk away feeling like they have a total and complete understanding of what you said. You are not in control of someone else's understanding and you are not the gatekeeper to Black knowledge. I like to think of our role as more of a supplement to whatever knowledge they have accumulated thus far. Something to bring life to what they've been learning or to provide helpful support to what they believe to be true based on your Black experience. We are the place they practice their knowledge and skills, which is how it should be. Those who want to be allies, who want to partner with communities different from their own, should move beyond what they've read or watched and apply it to actual relationships. This is such a key component because not everything you read or watch is the whole truth. Every book, podcast, or documentary you take in, comes from a very specific point of view that will never be the complete picture because none of us as individuals can ever represent an entire community in its totality. Not with the complexities that come with everyone's unique experiences, personalities, cultures, and the way that humanity is ever evolving. So, you can read all the books you want (including this one!), watch all the documentaries you want, and read all the articles, but if you truly want to understand Black people or anyone different than you, you have to seek out relationships too. Relationship is the key to putting what you've learned into practice, to confirm the validity of what you've learned, and to guard yourself from only rising to the point of being a scholar of diversity but not an actual proponent of it.

There are a lot of scholastic humanitarians out there. Those who can recite the history of slavery, and who know the intricacies of systemic racism, but when you look at their social circles - they consist primarily of people who look like them. This may be the case depending on where someone lives and whether it's a diverse community of people or not, but then you look at their social media feeds and it's a sea of sameness. You observe their everyday interactions and when presented with opportunities, big or small, to make connections with people different from them, they aren't present. Do they socialize with those who look different from them but only because they run in adjacent social circles as they do? Are they only from similar socioeconomic circles as them? Possibly. Are they friends with brown people that other people of sameness say are "good people"? Maybe. Do they donate to various charities that help marginalized people? They might. However, what I think is most important is how they show up for people that have nothing to offer them. How do they show up for people that they truly have nothing in common with?

It's unfortunate, but I have seen it too many times, specifically when it comes to the white community. There is a lot of good sounding diversity language being thrown around and yet the way they live their everyday life doesn't line up. Yes, this is the definition of hypocrisy, but we all practice hypocrisy in our lives, in one way or another, because of our imperfections. So why is this such a big deal? We're all only human, so why should we draw attention to these little inconsistencies? Well, for starters, because giving ourselves pass after pass for the way we only show up for people who make us feel the most comfortable, only when it's most convenient, and in ways that never really challenge our biases is part of the framework that racism, bigotry, and division is built on. You have to be diligent in self-awareness and continually press your comfort zones so that you don't eventually lull yourself into complacency. This is where, as the saying goes, "the proof is in the pudding". The proof of antiracist efforts isn't only in what you intellectually know, but it's in how willing you are to put yourself out there so you can turn concepts into connection.

This is where, as the Black community, we can come in as a supplemental source of information. For those who are trying to make the connection between what they know about Black people and what the actual Black experience is like from personal accounts, we can help. In this they will get actual snapshots of the diversity of Black life, which is something they will only be able to get a grasp of by sparking conversation with various people within the Black community. They need to speak and listen, they need to be curious, they need to be courageous, and they have to put themselves out there and give themselves permission to not have the answers in order to develop their allyship. We need to be open hearted and willing to listen. We need to try to match their curiosity to understand, with a desire to be understood. And when they take a step toward us to make connections, we should try to meet them halfway. This is one of many paths to being the change. As tempting as it may be not to bother with one another, missing an opportunity to connect when there is a lack of understanding reaps consequences that reach beyond the moment we have chosen to pass up. There are consequences that both parties will suffer, though in the immediate moment they may get to avoid an interaction that has the potential to feel uncomfortable, in the long term that avoidance benefits no one.

Let's take a moment to look at things from a point of view I think a large majority of the people reading this book will be able to relate to. It's safe to say that most of us have been students in a classroom setting at one point or another in our lives. We've all experienced those dreaded moments when the teacher asks the classroom a question, and it's met with dead silence and glazed stares. Either nobody cares or nobody feels confident in their answer. As someone who was not a great student in school, I was definitely one of those glazed stares! What do students do when they feel like their answers are stupid or they want to ask the teacher to explain what they mean but they don't want to feel like they're being annoying? They stop engaging. They shrink into themselves; they stop being curious, and they usually just go with whatever the people around them believe is right or what they're being

7

taught by someone else. That's what I did in school. People who feel too fearful or embarrassed to ask questions about what they don't know, cease to make genuine connections with others out of fear that their lack of understanding will be seen and held against them. They hold tight to assumptions, observations, and hearsay because they are safer than the risk of getting a response equal to the weight of their lack of confidence. This analogy rings true for so many, even beyond the topic of this book. No matter who you are, how old, what size, shape, or color you are, no one likes feeling stupid in front of people. Especially in front of people that you may already feel out of your element around because they aren't "your people". I've been there many times before. You've probably been there too, and I would dare to say we'll all be there again at some point in the future.

For those who have knowledge that would be beneficial to the person shying away from gaining understanding, they miss out on the chance to share their story. They don't get to be heard or bring their unique experiences to life in a way that could make a difference. There's also an assumption that's further cemented when they aren't being engaged, and that's the assumption that the other party just doesn't care. I've assumed this myself numerous times because, although the nice thing to do is to assume positive intentions, I'm not a mind reader! None of us are, so we only know what we're told, or we take a cue from the actions of others. If you've worked with me 5 days a week, 8 hours a day, for the past 10 years and have put little to no effort into asking me anything about myself or my life, I'm going to assume you just don't care. Even if you've been curious about my life, the reality is that your thoughts don't communicate like words do. And I don't know about you, but I'm the type that if you don't show an interest in me, I'm not going to just hand my life story over to you on a silver platter. Especially when I don't know where your head is. Intentional interest builds rapport. Consistent interest builds relationship. No interest means no connection and no change in anyone's biases or assumptions of who the other person is. So, do you see how both parties not showing up to the table leaves both hungry in one way or another? When we are all willing to surrender our ego and our fear in moments of sensitive conversations, we are doing much more than broadening each other's worldview. We are arming each other, even in the smallest of ways, with more confidence to make genuine connections with others different from ourselves. People who feel empowered to make genuine connections with those who aren't the same as them, become less fear driven and more curious. Curiosity leads to more open mindedness, and open mindedness leads to less judgement. Fear, close mindedness, and judgment are some of the major cornerstones of division. This is why our approachability and our willingness to show up for one another matters so much. Our stories matter. The good, the bad, and the ugly. It all matters and if spoken about in a way that enlightens one another, we can be empowered to speak our truth while also empowering someone else to gain some understanding of it.

Y'all, this is the deep work! This is about so much more than just feeding into biases we may have about each other. Like, "They're so stupid!" or "They're always so angry!" This is about being committed to being a part of each other's healing and feeling a self of responsibility for it. If you're Black you may be wondering "So you're expecting me to educate people just so they can feel less stupid? How does that help me?! What about the pain and confusion I've been through?" I hear you. I do. I know your hurt because I have felt it too. Even if our experiences may not be twins, our souls still scar the same, and this lesson in grace is one I'm leaning into as well.

I've learned through the various types of relationships in my life whether romantic, parental, friendship, or colleagues, a relationship that fosters a clearer understanding of one another is often the beginning of healing for both of us. When I feel understood, I feel safe. When I feel understood, I feel cared about. When I feel understood I feel braver. When I feel understood I feel more anchored to my authentic self. When I feel understood, I fear misunderstanding less and less. I recognize that misunderstanding is not always as personal as my pain makes it out to be. The more understanding I foster; the more misunderstandings lose their power and they simply become missed-understandings. They're simply an understanding that got missed somehow.

When you get lost and your GPS does that thing where it loses its mind for a moment and takes you off course, do you get annoyed? Sure! Do you throw up your hands and say "Well, I missed my exit because GPS said something stupid! Now I guess I'm just going to have to stay lost forever!!" No, of course not! What you end up doing in one way or another is just redirecting your course. The same can be true of our interactions where understanding is trying to be established. When you have a missed-understanding just redirect the conversation so that it's going back in the direction of

10

understanding. As with GPS, redirecting doesn't always get you to your destination in the same way you had previously planned. Sometimes getting there looks a little different than you imagined, but like travel there are many ways to get where you need to go. As long as you don't get so wrapped up in the fact that you got lost in the first place. Just redirect.

TWO - Living Beyond Definitions

I am by no means a historian, but you don't have to be in order to know that various forms of segregation have been going on in places around the world since the beginning of time. As humans feel this deep need to categorize and group people together, Social Categorization is something that psychologists have been studying in some way, shape, or form for decades. My experience with it is that we compartmentalize people groups in order to create order in our own minds. It helps us make sense of the complexities of humanity and to manage the mental chaos that can ensue when we feel there is just too much going on regarding how we are to interact with the world around us. Social Categorization isn't limited to race, but transcends to gender, age, occupation, and actually can be applied to any other trait associated with a person. I definitely encourage you to research the psychology behind it because it's actually very interesting, and although this isn't the book to do a deep dive into that research, it's definitely worth checking into.

With so many different types of people, with different

religious beliefs, philosophies, and various cultural back-grounds, things can get pretty overwhelming very quickly when trying to keep track of all the differences between them. It's understandable that it would be much easier and more convenient to lump all of a certain type of people together and define them as a whole, rather than take into consideration who they may be as an individual within the larger group. I mean, we are all guilty of doing this. Though it may be easier, any of us who have been generalized and categorized, based on the fact that we were the same race as so-and-so, or have had assumptions made about us because of one common trait as someone else, know the pain and frustration it can stir up depending on the context in which the commonality is being used. It can be belittling to feel like someone doesn't see you for who you are; apart from anyone else. After-all, the race you were born into, the culture you were raised in, the city you grew up in, and the way your parents raised you is not all that makes you. The older you get and the harder you work to forge your own way, the more you define who you are. I believe race, culture, and the way you were raised will most certainly influence how you relate to the world. However, to not take into consideration personal choice and evolution, is to take power from the human race and our capacity to live beyond definitions we were grandfathered into.

Consider for a moment the possibility that we, the Black community, or any minority community reading this, are not innocent in perpetuating similar biases onto people different from us. Now pause. Reread that sentence one more time and try to consider it without offense if you feel the "How dare she?" monster start to creep up inside of you. Is it possible that we could be taking something that may be a very natural part of humanity, something that people across cultures, races, socioeconomic statuses, and religious beliefs have all participated in, and are internalizing it as something that is specifically out to target us? Have we created an enemy out of all people different from us, based on them acting out a very natural part of human nature, no matter what the intent may be? A part of humanity that even we may be participating in against them? Are we as a community leaving space for, not just our humanity, but the humanity of all?

Why Don't You Date Black Guys?

At the numerous points in my life at which I had people ask me this question, I had technically never dated anyone Black. That is unless you counted the mixed boyfriend I had for like 2 months in middle school. But he hardly counts because middle school relationships are complete crap and I think the only interaction I had with him were make-out sessions at the roller rink and the occasional moments where we sat next to each other in the lunchroom. So other than him, I hadn't dated anyone Black until I reached my 30s.

I had grown up in a predominately white city, in white schools, white churches, a majority of my friends were white, and well, I think you get the picture. I know my experience of being a Black person with little other Black representation around them wasn't unique to only me. This is the story of many minorities in general, but for many years of my life I felt as if I was going through it alone. I wanted so desperately to feel more connected to my community, but creating that bond growing up was a journey on a road not well paved. My experience was constantly reinforced to me, by the Black community, that I wasn't Black enough in one way or another. Whether it was the way I spoke, the way I dressed, the way I walked, or what I ate. I tried. I really tried. If I'm honest there were times when I tried way too hard, which happens sometimes when you want something bad enough. I always felt like the community I should have had access to, based on the merit that I was Black, was this secret society that required a special handshake and code word to get into - but that no one would share with me. It was incredibly frustrating, but even more-so, it was very isolating. So, I made friends with, and dated whomever liked me, regardless of me being Black or not being Black enough.

When bringing up the lack of diversity in my love life to my non-Black friends I would always get a response of shock and awe. It usually sounded something like "WHAT?! Why don't you date Black guys? Even I've dated a Black guy before!" I would laugh outwardly but inwardly I was like "Well congratu-FRICKEN-lations to you!" Oftentimes it was just assumed that because I was Black, surely, I primarily only dated Black men. I always thought that was so interesting. It usually ended up becoming a much larger conversation, but I would explain that I have always dated whomever liked me for me. I thought it was just the way things should operate when it comes to finding love. That's the general consensus isn't it? To date whomever you click with, find attractive, and who has a mutual interest in you, right? For me at that time, it just hadn't yet been a Black guy. The funny thing is that the women questioning me weren't Black and yet had dated Black men themselves. I began wondering why it was always a question of why I didn't date Black men exclusively, but Black men weren't being challenged as to why they weren't dating Black women exclusively? I always thought that was so backwards, but never did I decide to challenge it.

Now that years have gone by since this question last puzzled me, I have a whole different perspective on those conversations and I have a much more transparent answer for why it is that I primarily ended up dating white men. Though a large portion of the truth is that I was almost exclusively surrounded by white men, that isn't the whole truth. The other portion of my truth is that I was actually kind of scared of and intimidated by Black men. I was intimidated because I didn't know them and didn't feel that I understood them. And I was scared because I had internalized my negative experiences as well as the experiences of "others". Who these "others" were, was debatable. Sometimes it was someone I knew personally, but a lot of times it wasn't. Regardless, my reluctance to them developed and it felt very real to me, as do most of our fears we convince ourselves are real.

I had almost exclusively only experienced disapproval from Black men, so I came to the conclusion that none of them thought I was pretty enough or Black enough. Majority of my experiences were with Black men that sexualized, cheated on, and degraded women, so I came to the conclusion that none of them respect the opposite sex. I witnessed Black men that were men of God at church and then were anything but Godly outside church walls, so I came to the conclusion that "Christian" Black men couldn't be trusted. The list goes on and on, unfortunately. I even internalized comments from family that expressed silly ideas about if a Black man was seen riding a bike it must be because he didn't have a car, and so I created a story that every Black man riding a bike down the street must not have any money! These were my biases about Black men – yes, from a Black woman. Of course, I shake my head in disbelief at myself now. I'm embarrassed by how I perpetuated such racist ideas toward Black men. Now, maybe to you, hearing me calling my thoughts racist might be a little harsh. I mean, it's not like I hated Black men. I was however completely suspicious of every single one of them no matter who they were.

So yes, I would call my ideas racist. I created my stories based on what other people told me, on how the media often portrayed them as criminals and degenerates, and on the experiences that were made up of my little world in Michigan. And I used them as weapons against all Black men everywhere. That is sadly racism at its finest. It is exactly what has formed the opinions and supports the very violence that we see from everyday people, some law enforcement, and even many facets of our government, to people of color. It hurts me to know that these very ideas I had, told me investing time and energy into understanding Black men was a moot point. Surely, they didn't actually care about showing up in the world in a positive way, and these were the same ideas that killed George Floyd and Elijah McClain.

Black women were a whole other source of contention for me, filled with a different set of stories that were just as detrimental. The majority of Black females I met compared my blackness to theirs and I never measured up, so I assumed that all Black women thought they were better than me. The majority of my interactions with Black women were doused in hostility before I could even make a good case for who I was, and so I assumed most Black women had attitudes and would hate me before we even got a chance to know each other. The stories go on and on and are really more of the same. You see, the story I told myself, of why I didn't have a strong tie to the Black community wasn't admitted in full truth to myself for a long time. Not because I was consciously trying to live a lie, but because I just didn't understand the dynamics that were being played out inside me. I didn't understand the full dynamics of my relationship with the Black community, because I didn't understand my own biases yet. Since I didn't see my biases, I couldn't question them or even challenge how I was discrediting thousands of Black people based on the small worldview I had at the time. A view that didn't reach outside the boundaries of my primarily white town.

It wasn't right and it wasn't fair, but at the time ignorantly lumping everyone together just made sense. In my small world, majority experience ruled and I think that's the trap so many fall into. We let what has been the majority of our experience rule an entire worldview, even if our world only consists of our family and church group, or the city we've lived in our whole life. The reality is that with people we are afraid of, we come to conclusions about them that we don't automatically come to with other people. Black men were not the only men who talked down to me, there were other men who did that too, but I didn't conclude that they all thought I wasn't good enough. Black women weren't the only ones who communicated to me that I wasn't good enough, there were other women who did that too, but I didn't conclude that they all hated me. This is the deceptive logic of racism at work and this is why I'm putting myself out here as an example of how you can perpetuate it even within your own community.

Honestly, I have gone back and forth about how transparent I should be about my journey. On one hand I want anyone out there who needs it, to know that they are not alone. On the other hand, I just want to protect myself from any cruelty and unbridled judgement. Yet I know it's important that if we are going to talk about racism, we cannot exclude the fact that Black people can be racists too. We can be racist to others, as well as to each other, sometimes without even seeing it for what it really is.

I've been ashamed, but I do not live in that shame. That's how I can talk to you about it now. I'm grateful for the evolution that can come with maturity, the intentional pursuit of challenging our comfort zones, and the growth that can come when we choose to humble ourselves and become lifelong learners. The idealist in me just wants to give the entire world a magic pill, then sit back and watch in awe as the emotional and psychological chains shackling us all to our biases about one another, turns to dust. However, there is no magic pill now is there? There's only effort. Effort made intellectually by you and I. Since it doesn't hurt to dream, hypothetically, if there was a magic pill I could give you that would help to heal this great divide, would you take it? If I could guarantee that this magic pill would be the solution to all the misunderstanding, the ignorance, the assumptions, the violence, and the biases, would you be the first one lined up at the door? Would you drink down all that Martin Luther King

Jr. had a vision of achieving and even beyond his wildest dreams? Or could it be that this divide has become like a warm glass of milk that we drink to ease us into a comfortable slumber? I just wonder.

THREE - Flip the Script

Having knowledge is hard work. You know why? Because knowledge is an accountability partner. The more of it you have, the more it reminds you that you can do better. The more of it you have, the harder it is to say you didn't know what was required of you without having to squeeze past your conscience to do it.

I started a 6-month program with Johan, a dear friend and executive coach in January, 2020. At the time I'm writing this chapter, I only have 1 month left to participate in, and it has been the most rewarding personal growth experience I've had to date. When I first opened to the idea of this coaching program, I had thoughts of what this experience was going to be like. I had financial goals in mind that I wanted to meet. I was hoping to get some insight into how to create an advancement plan at my job. And in general, I was hoping to spark a new level of motivation. Basically, I was looking for him to be a hybrid of my personal hype-man and my Pinterest quotes board! It was the largest financial investment into myself that I had ever made, so that was a huge leap, in and of itself. I went into it thinking of that sweet 20k in additional income I wanted to make, and a plan for how to work from home more. What I got was more than I bargained for, but everything I didn't know I needed. I got a clearer picture of who I really was: A scared woman living within a little box that I built by hand and on the doormat leading into it read "Welcome to my comfort zone. Stay awhile".

Let me start by saying that Johan and I had been friends for a of couple years at the point I expressed my interest in coaching with him. And though it might seem strange that I would want to start an executive coaching relationship with a friend, it didn't at all feel like an odd thing to do. He's a motivational speaker, an author, and all around beautiful human being whom I have a lot of admiration for. Besides, I trusted that his coaching style would fit my personality, which is half the battle when attempting to find a coach or mentor that you click with. When we set up a date for an intake call, I was pretty pumped about it! That was until the intake form to prep for the call landed in my inbox. I eagerly opened the email expecting to see questions such as "Where do you want to be in 5 years?" And "Name your top 5 strengths and weaknesses". Instead, however, there were things like "What is the hardest thing in your life that you've had to overcome?" And "List five things that you are tolerating or putting up with in your life at present". Then the motherload of questions "If you reach the age of 95 and continue to live your life and order your time the way you are right now, what regrets do you think you will have?" I went through this entire intake form, read every question with bated breath, and then immediately went into panic mode. I thought "Nope. No. Not a chance. There's no way I'm going to do this. He's going to know too much about me and this is not what I signed up for!" Yep. That was my first reaction. Fear that I would become known. Fear that someone I wanted to impress would realize I'm far from impressive and would be disappointed to get to know the woman I truly was. Fear of having someone witness how truly unraveled I was on the inside. Fear of confronting all of the things I've masked with smiles, sarcasm, and all those Pinterest quotes. That intake form was the beginning of me confronting my fear of being understood.

Since I've already revealed that I'm a month away from completing the program, you don't have to guess that I didn't let that fear (no matter how overwhelming it felt at times) keep me from taking this leap of faith, but that doesn't mean that the fear ended there, far from it actually. It just took on new forms as, over time, with every kind but direct invitation from Johan to take a deeper look into the stories I've told myself, and with every conscious decision I made to show up to each session determined to get what he called "Max value", the fear got smaller and smaller until it no longer became the first thing I clung to when I felt like I was sinking. As my fear got smaller, my sense of personal ownership got bigger.

You see, I'm 36 years old and I could no longer blame my parent's perceived lack of ambition in life for the reason I found myself giving up on things quickly. Like "I get bored easily" was no longer a valid reason. No longer could I blame my ex's failed attempts at being the man I needed him to be, as the reason I hadn't dated in years. No longer could I blame my employer's lack of flexible schedule options as the reason I just assumed I'd never have the freedom to work from home so that I could travel more often. I'm a grown woman who, just like everyone else, has been fighting since birth for independence and an opportunity to step into their individuality. Yet, when I arrived at this coveted destination in life as an adult, even with my own space, paying my own cable bill, and not having anyone to tell me that Dove chocolates and popcorn are not an acceptable dinner, inwardly I still defaulted to the limiting beliefs that I inherited from my family. The mindsets I developed as a result of some guy who didn't value himself enough to value me, and ideas from friends that were often walking around in the dark just as I was. I was an adult who had the possibility of creating any narrative I wanted and yet I continued to rewrite the same chapters over and over again with only the hero and the villain changing. The sad part is, I wasn't even giving myself a leading role in my own story! I wasn't the hero or the villain. I was the person watching the two battle it out to the death from the sidewalk. But hey, at least I was passionate about witnessing the fight. I stood on the sidelines yelling "That's right! Get him! Take him out! Don't let him talk to you like that!!" And well... that's about it. I was all passion and very little action.

I wonder where in life you might be showing up like this? Very passionate about the issue of racial division, discrimination, and injustice, but not actually following through on your sense of personal responsibility for how you can affect it in your world? I wonder in what ways you avoid being understood by someone different than you or gaining understanding of the narratives you've created, because to do so would mean there's the possibility of another truth out there. That maybe you have something to contribute in this important fight other than you validating the stories of other people's lives. That maybe it's time you wrote some new stories.

"I Heard Black Girls Do It Best"

While on a date....

> Guy: "So I heard Black girls do it best. Is that true?"
> Me, clearly confused: "You heard Black girls do WHAT the best?"
> Guy: "Sex"
> Me *enter cringing emoji*: "Umm, sooo, wait. DO you or DON'T you want to share the calamari?"

(Don't judge - a girls gotta eat, and it's calamari over everything, alright?)

Let's just say that was the last time I ever went out with that dude and it wasn't just because I was like, "Bro, maybe that's one of those things you say after we've gone out on a few dates and now I like you too much to notice that it's a questionable thing to say!" I didn't go out with him again because it quickly became clear as the night went on that he went out with me because he was aiming to find out if this theory that the big "they" told him was true. Unfortunately for him the only thing he found out is that I was not the one, honey! I am not a social experiment that someone can play around with. This is not one of those "If you hear a tree fall in the forest..." things but instead "If you have sex with a Black girl..." because last I knew my caramel vagina works the same as the vanilla, or other ones do.

My date was just another unfortunate casualty of misinformation by ingestion. He drank the Kool Aid and he swallowed what somebody else fed him. I can only speculate, but his source could have been a buddy that had sex with a Black girl once and had his mind blown, a movie that depicted Black women as insatiable and down for whatever, or he could just be watching too much Love & Hip Hop or porn. Who knows? Unfortunately, he's not the only guy I've encountered that, usually based on tv or hip-hop lyrics, assumed I was some kind of nympho who had no sexual boundaries at all and was down for whatever, whenever. I think this perception is both prevalent within the Black community just as much as it is outside out it.

TV, movies, music videos, porn, they all create a precedent that no Black woman asked for or promised to align ourselves with. It's reflected in the sexual expectations that are set on Black women every day. Men see it when they see us. Women too. With men it seems more overt, more obvious. The images are cemented into our lives in ways that you may not even initially notice until it's brought to your attention that it's happening. The images of Black women twerking on the hood of cars, in the middle of large groups of men, or the way Black women are often depicted as craving or thriving off cat-calling. More often we see images of other women turning their noses up to cat-calling or even standing up for themselves. However, Black women are often shown as walking down the street, random men yelling to them what they want to do to them as they walk by, and yet what's shown? A Black woman doing a little coy side smile, a hair flip, and walking with a strut in her step. In fact, I would even go as far as to say there are instances in which, as a Black woman, if you don't appear accepting of the lewd comments of Black men, you are almost made to feel as if you are betraying the Black community by not obliging.

That is the culture that has been created for us, the one many choose to recreate. This is the role many have played. It is solidified with every mention or image connected to Black women in which we're painted to crave attention any way we can get it, no matter which way it's given to us or is to the detriment of our personal power. Now maybe you're thinking "Girl I cannot relate because I'm strong, powerful, and I know I am a Queen worthy of respect!" And if that's you, I applaud you and as much as you may be woke about yourself, this is not every woman's experience. When you look across the board of all women of every shade you will see that what may seem like the common sense of a woman's worth to you, is not all that common for everyone else. For every time you require a man to respect you there are at least 2 women who smiled and felt flattered by his unsolicited advances. Every positive reaction to that man's come-ons only help support his belief that his behavior is acceptable. I like to think of it as every time I react favorably to a man's degrading behavior toward me, I unintentionally support his degrading of women I don't know and the degrading of all of the young girls I haven't met. That just hits a little too hard for me to be okay with letting certain interactions slide.

I also see the sexualization of Black women played out in other ways that aren't connected to sexual-harassment or attention given to you that depreciates your value. I've seen it in the biases associated with the sensuality of Black women. I have witnessed and experienced the presence of a Black woman being interpreted as a kind of sensual predator in certain social settings. Like when a single Black woman enters a room where there may be primarily white couples, and you watch otherwise relaxed women sit up straighter and magically the gap between them and their significant other closes rather quickly in her presence. Then there's the Black woman in the workplace who wears a pencil skirt, not different from other women. Yet the way it lays against her curves gets the reaction of raised eyebrows as if having hips was a crime. These are not cases of overt racism. Of course not. That would be looked down upon swiftly. These are quiet biases. Like the apps that continue to run on your phone in the background even when not in use. These biases run in the back of your mind without you really even processing them and then show up in tiny ways that are often dismissed or not even noticeable enough for you to make the conscious decision to look past them. They show up in the way you reach for your boyfriend's hand when you see a Black woman enter the room. It's evident in the thought that passes your mind when you see a Black woman wearing a bright color or a "flashy" piece of jewelry and you subconsciously think she's just trying to get attention. It's in the way you question the intentions of any Black woman that shows a simple kindness to a man that is not her man. These quiet biases pull out all the stealthy moves in our minds and easily get away with it day after day, if gone unchecked.

In what ways are biases running in the background of your mind in your day-to-day life when you see a picture of, speak to, or stand next to "them"? Whoever "them" may be. We all have a "them". I wonder how many of those biases go unchecked, building upon the one before, like bricks stacked on top of one another, cemented together by mortar until it has built a wall so high it keeps you from seeing the person on the other side of your assumptions...a human being...a soul dressed in flesh.

FOUR - The Diversity of Racism

Oftentimes when we think of a racist, or of prejudice, the image that comes to mind is that of an angry person. We see them moving through life with hatred in their hearts, scowling at every person different from them, mistreating those they are racist against. In general, you may believe you can sniff out a racist because racists are bad people that ooze negativity. This, however, is far from the truth, even though I completely get why this opinion is formed. The image of a racist has been connected with the image of the KKK and people on videos that go viral where they are ruthlessly beating people in the streets. The images of racists are of people who wear hatred on their face, in their body language, and even on their person by way of a symbol. But do not be fooled. These ideas of what racism looks like only help to create a false safety that makes us all believe if we're not beating people in the streets, if we're generally a happy person, if we're not yelling out racist slurs, then there's no way we could possibly be a racist or be prejudiced. It's painting a picture in which you can compare yourself with an extreme,

33

and in most cases, you will naturally not find yourself in the same exact group as an extreme because extremes are by definition when you've reached the highest point of something! So, unless you are the leader of the KKK, or you've murdered someone simply because of the color of their skin, or because of any other distinctive characteristics of theirs, it will be very easy for you to craft an opinion of yourself that you definitely have no racist tendencies because you have never, and could never be like "those people". However, I'd like to invite you to challenge yourself on this. Not because you might be a racist without knowing it, but to challenge the internal dialogue we have with ourselves about what racism might look like in action in the world today. In general, racism is widespread and known to be detrimental, yet the signs of it are not always loud. Sometimes they are more like ripples. Subtle, at first, yet far reaching.

Since I'm a woman who loves metaphors, let me paint a picture for you that I think a majority of us can relate to. Imagine putting yourself on a diet in efforts to lose weight and you've been good during the week by sticking to the plan. Then, on the weekend you go to McDonald's and eat 2 quarter pounders with cheese. If someone were to call you out for going off your diet because they witnessed you stuffing your face in the car that you parked in the farthest deep dark corner of the McDonald's parking lot, what would your response to them be? Personally speaking, I would probably sheepishly say something like "Yes, I'm on a diet but I had a craving!" or "Yes I'm on a diet but I was good all week so I felt like I deserved a treat!" And the reality is that regardless of my burger binge, at the end of the day I would still consider myself on a diet because I know I don't make a habit of stuffing my face like that every day. Though this wouldn't be everyone's logic, it's definitely been mine when I've gone on diets!

Well racism and prejudice for the majority of people who aren't an extreme can be a lot like the person who's on a diet, has a cheat day, but still technically considers themselves on a diet. Racism can be very similar in that you don't have to do, or say, racist or prejudiced things every day in order to still have racism in your heart. You could have gone the whole week without paying much attention to anyone and then on a Saturday afternoon someone cuts you off in traffic, now you're pissed and you notice it's a minority male driving the vehicle. You exclaim, "He wasn't even paying attention! Probably because he couldn't hear me above his rap music and if he'd sit up straight and be more concerned with his driving than being a thug maybe he would have seen me coming." Well, that escalated quickly, now didn't it? The reality is that this kind of thing happens to us more often than we care to admit. We're going along in life, doing our thing, not a conscious prejudiced thought in our minds, and then BOOM, we have some kind of experience with one of "those people". Then we vomit up all the assumptions, biases, bigotry, and hate that were just simmering below the surface. It only came to a boil when the heat got cranked.

Don't misunderstand the goal here. This isn't about trying to convince someone they're a racist. This is about prompting you to consider the diversity of prejudice and all of the many ways it can show up within ourselves. Just because your prejudiced acts aren't frequent doesn't mean there's not some kind of racism being played out in your life. If we are going out into the world saying we believe everyone is the same and we just "can't believe that in today's world people are still racist" then progress starts with us challenging ourselves and asking ourselves if there are areas where we need to show up better in, or get healing from. It starts with us tuning into those thoughts, words, or emotions that rise to the surface when we encounter triggering situations or people. Really, the overarching question here is: Who are you when you're not controlling who you want other people to see?

As there are those who are in the process of self-auditing their biases or privilege, many have expressed how guilty they feel for being ignorant of their biases and of the reality of racism. Currently many people have no choice but to see the hatred they had otherwise turned a blind eye to and are questioning if there has been any role they have played in the suppression of Black people. Now we all know there's a difference between seeing something as wrong and doing something about it. But unless you are both blind and deaf, avoidance in this moment is futile. The thing about guilt is that it can become deceptively addictive. It has a way of making you believe that guilt, in and of itself, is an act of change when in fact, it is not. Oftentimes guilt shows up in our lives as an emotional response to an intellectual acknowledgement of our own lack of integrity in a certain area in our lives. Guilt is usually just a signal that we should do better. It's a precursor to change, but it is not the change itself. If you're not careful you can find yourself settling in the cycle of guilt and feeling tied to it by the entitlement that says "I should be congratulated for feeling guilty because bad people don't feel guilt, but I do".

This is why it's crucial that while you are on your journey of awareness and of becoming anti-racist, it's important that you seek out people who will partner with you to challenge your own biases and create community. There can be a danger that comes from starting your journey and yet keeping the same company of people who take being challenged on their biases as a form of personal victimization. Although I'm optimistic that growth is still possible, if you are truly sold on it, I would be lying if I said I didn't believe you were at risk of reverting back to comfortable ways. Community brings energy to our beliefs. That's why churches are such a pivotal part of Christianity, why AA groups are an important part of the sobriety journey, and why there are some kind of support groups for every interest out there. A part of inundating yourself with the hobby, idea, sport, or religion is to surround yourself with not only resources that further substantiate your interest, but people that can provide you with real life examples of what it looks like to really be all in. Just as watching sports on TV at home alone will never have the same energy as you being at the stadium surrounded by people who are as passionate about the game as you are. Building community with those who are also proponents of change will serve to take the interest you already have and energize it. Bias and prejudice get their power from the comradery that forms with people who create community together based on their shared lack of knowledge or intentional decision not to seek understanding. Those of us who want to be the bridge in this great divide amongst communities should also do the same and even more intentionally.

"You speak very articulately."

Usually when you are the only Black person or minority of any kind in a room, it's expected that you will be studied. Yes, you heard me right. Studied. Like a work of abstract art that people find intriguing, unfamiliar, and oftentimes just outside the reach of their understanding. You may have an idea of its interpretation but you'll never fully know the story behind it unless you speak to the artist who created it. Being different in a world where you are surrounded primarily by those bound together by their sameness, feels much like being a piece of art on a wall in front of onlookers. The number of times I have had experiences where I am literally treated as if I'm a very rare Picasso that everyone just discovered existed, are too many to count. Whether it was in church, in the workplace, in bars, or standing in line at the post office, I've experienced the curious and analytical stares of people that just don't know what to do with me. I'm lighter skinned which throws people off who have a limited concept of the shade spectrum of the Black community. They feel like I may be too light skinned to be fully Black. Maybe she's mixed? I open my mouth to say something, and in some instances, jaws literally almost drop to the ground like "She can't possibly be totally Black. She must be mixed because she talks like a white person". Then throw into the mix when I'm wearing a certain kind of weave or wig which results in people thinking I'm Latina, and I've also been asked if I was Hawaiian. So, you see Black and brown people are not only coming up against prejudice and racism, but we also have to deal with consciously or subconsciously being mistaken as interchangeable for some other brown person just because we share similar skin tones or other traits. These seemingly small things, built up over time, can often leave people of color feeling like our identity is being painted over so something more understandable can be created out of it.

I have actually had people disagree with me when I tell them I am Black. They've actually just flat out said, "No you're not. You couldn't be. Are you sure you're not mixed?" Yes, people actually have the nerve to tell other people what their race or ethnicity is! This is a real thing that happens and it's baffling. Yet, sadly enough I'm used to it. How sad is that? Most people of color are used to a plethora of somethings when it comes to having to suppress our race, ethnicity, or culture, or having to almost bargain with people on how much of it will be allowed in certain spaces. Most people of color are used to microaggressions like this, and yes, someone telling me that I couldn't possibly be Black is a microaggression. When someone says this to me it's as if they're telling me that I couldn't possibly be Black because Black people act and look a certain way that fits their idea of what Black people are, and since I don't fit that same mold, I must have another identity that makes more sense to them. These same people would be so offended to be called prejudiced or racists, but that sure as heck isn't anti-racist behavior. When by your words, you are trying to take someone's identity away from them so that it fits the identity you desire them to have, what do you call that? Being told what I just "couldn't be" is one of thousands of examples of prejudices that can rear their ugly heads. At the time, I hadn't yet found my voice and was still afraid of letting all that made me uniquely me, including my Blackness, take center stage. So, I placed my Blackness as an understudy to the role that everyone around me could most easily identify with and the role that would get me the standing ovation. You would think that after years of the same consistent attention I'd get used to it...unfortunately, for the most part, I did get used to it. I had been used to it, yet the interesting thing is that I also ended up usually feeling surprised by it. It just never failed that if there had ever been a moment where I might have forgotten I was different; others would very readily remind me that I indeed was. Or that the parts of me that didn't fit their idea of being Black would be reimagined for me and presented to me as a much better option. I'm still used to it, but I'm no longer content with it. No one's identity should be up for debate. It's the one thing that a person truly has ownership of and it should stay in their possession.

Years ago, when I worked in the nonprofit world, I did public speaking with an organization that used to provide funding for the agency I worked at. This pro bono gig would land me in corporations, schools, factories, and wherever else there was thought to be people who would be willing to support the community with donations. I would speak about the agency I worked for and about the organization that supported us with funding and why the financial gifts of those listening touch more lives than they could imagine. I shared compelling stories of those whose lives were touched by the donations received.

I shared a small part of my story and how my personal life had been touched by the dollars they donated to this organization. I prompted those listening to me to remember that the names and faces of those touched by their donations might be their own one day, or their friends, or their families. To think about, if it were one of their loved ones that depended on the funding that came from this organization, would they urge people to give? In front of these people, who were using some of their lunch break to attend this presentation, or were actually being made to come when they had no interest in coming, I made it my mission to prompt a thought process that reached beyond the living breathing nonprofit infomercial I was in at that moment. I figured if I couldn't inspire their wallets, I could at least try to inspire their hearts.

After the presentation was done and when whomever was in leadership gave the word that people were free to leave, more often than not, most people wasted no time getting the heck out of the one place they didn't want to be at in the first place. However, of the few that stuck around to snag a couple of donuts to go or who chose to linger a little longer to buy time before having to go back to work, there would always be a handful that would come up to me to shake my hand or say thank you for coming. Of these few more than half of them would comment about how well I spoke. In any normal situation such as this it wouldn't seem like a big deal to get comments about it, but they didn't give any remarks about how they thought the content of the speech was quality. They didn't share what really spoke to them, and they didn't express that they discovered something new they didn't know before. The sentiment was always about how clearly I spoke, how articulate I was, or they wondered where I went to school based on how "well spoken" I was. When they asked me how

I came about the speaking opportunity, they'd respond to my answer with "Oh, well, good for you! That's very impressive. You should be proud of yourself!" or something to that effect, followed by an approving pat on the back. Always with the back pats. This was the typical response I would get from primarily white professionals and I couldn't help but wonder "What exactly did they expect?" And yet, I already knew very well what they were expecting, hence the expressions of amazement that I had often received as if the way I communicated was some kind of parlor trick that they were trying to figure out the secret of my achievement to. Every place I've ever worked there has been some kind of interaction where I'm treated as if meeting a Black professional is like coming in contact with a unicorn.

You see, there is a stereotype when it relates to how Black people should talk and this stereotype has been in place since the days of slavery. It was common knowledge that if you were a slave who was educated or you were discovered trying to acquire education in any way, you were posed as a threat. You would most likely be beaten into submission as a reminder that you could not and will not be equal to white people no matter if you could read, write, or articulate yourself. Though today, education in so many forms is available to us all, and though there are many Black men and women empowering the world with their minds and talents, there is still an air of mystery in many circles when it comes to Black people who express themselves in any way other than what's so often depicted as the only way to "sound black".

Many of us use, have heard of, mocked, or imitated ebonics in one way, shape, or form. Its influence is weaved into the way we consume entertainment, is a part of pop culture, and is of course a part of Black culture. I find it funny though, that of all the diversity one can see in the world today, there is still a level of surprise around the diversity of the Black community and the way we communicate. There is still a level of surprise when we don't all align ourselves with what is expected of us, based on characters on TV shows that play us. They base it on what has been summarized via experiences that people have had with other Black people, or based on what has been passed down through the rumor mill. Worse yet, it is based on what the news media highlights of the Black community. So often when met with someone of the Black community who doesn't align with what they pictured in their minds there seems to be a small implosion that happens. When a Black person strays from the image that is so stereotypically portrayed, they are met with, "Where did you come from? Are you full Black? Are you from Detroit? But are your parents from here?" We're met with speculation instead of celebration. What's more is that "articulation" is often seen as synonymous with education. If you're articulate that means you're educated. If you speak with "dis" and "dat" or reflect anything that's reminiscent of rap lyrics, they assume you are uneducated. Just like in anyone else, a person's dialect or accent can vary based on where they grew up, how those around them spoke, and what they choose to identify with. This is the case for us all! There are multiple layers of diversity within diversity. Education has nothing to do with it. Often many of us equate education with communication style, when they are not at all synonymous.

The stereotypes associated with how you communicate

have been a consistent source of discussion in my life in general, including my interactions with other Black people. Growing up in Holland, Michigan which is known for its Dutch culture and influence, it often felt as if not being Dutch made me an immigrant in the very town I had known all my life. I know there were other minorities who lived in the community and who shared a similar sentiment. It was also my experience that I felt like an immigrant around other Black people too. With the white community I was too brown, too thick, my hair was too different, and with the Black community I was too light, too "white", and too "country" (another way of saying I seemed to have more white attributes than Black). The way I communicated was perceived by many of the Black people I had interactions with growing up, as a sign that I must have thought I was better than them. Anytime I used a word or phrase that wasn't typical verbiage for a teen or that might have seemed a little mature for my age, I was deemed too white. Every time I was seen with another white student that went to my school; I was berated as if I was a deserter of war. It was my normal to not ever truly feel like I was enough for anyone, so in turn it translated to me not feeling enough for myself as a Black person for the majority of my life up until I reached my late 20s.

Limitations on who a person is, based on the way they speak, can come from all sides and could easily be considered one of the sneakiest kinds of biases that a person may have subconsciously and could go unchecked until it is challenged. Have you ever used the wrong word in a sentence before, or mispronounced something which totally affected the way you were trying to communicate an idea? Have you ever had those moments where you're in the middle of an argument and then all of a sudden you lose your footing and can't think of the word you want to use to get your point across? How about, have you ever shot off a quick text in which you used "your" when you should have used "you're"? In those instances where you didn't communicate yourself in exactly the way that was deemed appropriate or correct according to certain standards, I wonder what it might feel like for you if people made the assumption based off any of these instances that this was a clear indicator that you were uneducated, unintelligent, unmotivated to put your best foot forward, incapable? I wonder what harm those judgements might do to you? Maybe if it was once in a while it wouldn't bother you too much, I mean, you're only human after all. You might just think "Geez people lighten up it's not that serious!" Or maybe you'd just get defensive and would think "Screw them if they're going to make a big deal out of that, like they've never made a mistake before!" You may also notice that the mistakes and slip ups make you hyper aware to make sure you go through your texts and emails with a fine-tooth comb. Or you are a little slower to speak because you want to make sure you use the right words so you don't sound stupid. These instances that might happen once in a while, start to add up, affecting how you relate to the world and how you see yourself. Well, amplify all of that by much more and over the course of one's entire lifetime, for many people of color who don't fit into the box of what some think intelligence should sound like, it's disconcerting at best.

This chapter could go on and on with more examples, both subtle and exaggerated, of biases and assumptions that help support racist propaganda. There is, as I titled this chapter, such a thing as the diversity of racism. It's diverse in the ways we may knowingly or unknowingly participate in it and it's as diverse as the faces of those who practice it. There is a diversity of racism, but there is only one way to overpower it in our own lives. As we work to be the change, we must be overtly anti-racist. We are all more than the way people filter our potential and capacity for greatness through their own biases, experiences, and hatred. We are minds, hearts, souls, hopes, dreams, tears, hurts, and experiences, and every one of us deserves to not only thrive in our distinctives, but also be celebrated for them.

FIVE - Light Privilege

I've been telling lies for a long time. I've stuck to my story, rehearsed it, memorized my lines, and played such a believable character that I had almost fooled everyone, including myself. I've been telling lies. At no point in my life have I ever suffered from the majority of the intense displays of racism and prejudice as my darker skinned brothers and sisters have suffered and continue to suffer. I have been allowed to walk in circles that many of my darker skinned brothers and sisters have not been welcomed. I have been given allowances that many of my darker skinned brothers and sisters have been denied. I felt proud of this. I felt proud of this attention because I misunderstood what it meant to be the exception. I lied to myself and I lied to those perpetuating their biases through me by enabling the projection of an image of something that wasn't actually there. Like a hologram concert in which people pay money to be entertained essentially by the idea of someone who wasn't actually there to represent themselves. I was a hologram figure of Blackness in the homes of many white people for many years. I lied to us both. I lied to them by letting them believe they were okay because they let ME in, they listened to ME, they invited ME over for dinner, they let ME watch their children. I lied to myself every time I entertained someone I knew was prejudiced and treated other Black people with contempt. All the while making an exception for me because my shade of brown felt less threatening, more digestible, and more identifiable. It essentially could be pulled off as a darker shade of white. The shade that white women lay out under the hot sun for hours to get.

I lied to myself by believing that I represented all Black people and if they accepted me, then I made a point...that Black people aren't nearly as segregated as we claim to be. I lied to myself so well that I didn't realize my light privilege was showing.

I lived a life of trying to prove a point to the Black community. That we are no longer limited. That we are the ones placing limitations on who we could be, where we could go, and how we could live. That the shackles we are currently bound with no longer had a key belonging to our master but that it had been fully laid into the palm of our own hands to set ourselves free. That all we needed to do was rise above the oppression of the past and forge a new future. Any time I walked into a room of primarily white people with minimal stares I inwardly said "See! It's not so bad." Any time I went into a store with minimal supervision from a sales clerk I would inwardly say "See! I didn't get much more attention than anyone else in this store did, I'm sure." Any time a white male would show romantic interest in me I'd inwardly say "See! The world is changing!" That was my light privilege showing. I was so deep in white culture, white community, white privilege, and I was so committed to my desire to feel a part of a community, to be accepted, to trust who I inherently was, that I became desensitized to the diversity of the Black experience. That my Black life was not the representation of all Black lives. The crazy thing is that, subconsciously, I already knew this to be the case! If only I were to have even considered the stories of my family, where they recounted enduring pure hatred and mistreatment because they were Black within our primarily white community.

If I only would have considered the various ways Black people were still being murdered - just because they were Black. If I had given more attention to the examples of racism that I experienced by the hands of teachers who abused their power, I would like to believe that I couldn't have possibly considered people making an exception for me a form of flattery or a show of good faith that they weren't prejudiced. I would like to think that I would have been more aware than I actually was, but that had not been the case. The reality is that there had been a disconnect between me and the community that was in my blood from the time I was born. I could rattle off numerous ways in which I didn't have access to the broader Black community while growing up. Why my Black influence only spanned as far out as the small amount of people in my family. Why I didn't have genuine Black friendships until adulthood. Why I felt segregated from the community I wanted nothing more than to be welcomed by (some of the reasons I've expressed earlier in the book), but I'm not going to bore you with the details, because none of that even matters now. When you're young, you live how you were conditioned to live, but when you're an adult you have the ability to live the life you choose. As an adult the excuse "That's just how I was raised" and "I've always been this way" won't hold up in court and it doesn't hold up in life anymore either.

I am empathetic to how it's so easy for many of us to lean heavily on how we were raised as the reason for our habits or worldview. Whether helpful or hurtful, navigating what community looks like to you while growing up can be tough to say the least. This is especially true if you find yourself growing up in the midst of dysfunction and turmoil, or you lack the presence of discerning parental figures or mentors. There comes a time in your young life when you feel the pressure of being deeply assimilated into the community you were raised. Meanwhile, you're trying to figure out which community you believe in, apart from what you've been taught. We've all been there, at that delicate place in your development as a young person where you want nothing more than the ability to think for yourself. At the same time, you want nothing more than to be accepted for being the same. It's not unusual for young people to not want to be different from other people in their community because difference is often ostracized and as a young person there is nothing that hits harder than when you become a casualty of popular opinion. This balance is tough at any age, really. Even as adults there is a constant ebb and flow of wanting to fit in and wanting to buck the system. One of the things that makes that balance harder to achieve when you're a person of color is that there is no hiding from the fact that you are different from other people - you wear your difference on your skin.

There is no "I'll just go along with the program for now so no one suspects a thing until I'm out of this town and away from these people!" No, there is no escaping your differentiator. You are just stuck in your difference and there is no fooling other people into thinking you're right if they, the majority, have any assumptions of you being wrong based on your difference. You may be able to lull people into feeling safer around you by not challenging their biases, by avoiding the topic of your differences, or by mimicking them, but at the end of the day your skin tone will always give you away. That's what took me longer to accept because that acceptance has always had its limitations and costs, as a person of color in America. There will be no assimilation into the white community without being required to, in some way, suppress integral parts of who you are and to deny your family and your history. So, every day we are faced with the choice of, we will do our best to fly under the radar, or live out our truth at the expense of, in some very real ways not only our acceptance, but even our safety.

Though I may speak primarily on the topic of having to make choices every day to either assimilate or live our truth and take numerous risks in doing so as it refers to the Black experience and people of color, this truth is not just ours. It's the truth of anyone who is not a straight white person. Those in the LGTBQ+ community are faced with these same choices every day. To live their truth and take very real risks, or to assimilate in order to preserve the comfort of others by fracturing themselves to fit in. Those who have a disability that cannot be hidden or those with a mental illness that affects their lives every day and cannot be concealed from those around them are faced with choices too. Though the degree of these choices and the degree of risk may vary amongst us all, we all in some way and at various points in our life approach the crossroads where we ask ourselves, how much of who we are do we want to compartmentalize or suppress in order to be treated like we're not different? It's a devastating fact of the lives of those who are different, that many of sameness or "normalcy" might never fully understand the plight of. It's so easy for those of privilege to say "Just be yourself! Who cares!" when they don't ever have to make the choice between being themselves or putting themselves in harm's way. For some people and in certain situations, it is quite literally a choice between one or the other. Those who have the privilege of easily blending in at most places and can usually look around to find that they are surrounded by people who look like them, may feel unhindered in saying "Who cares what people think. You have to live your truth". It's a nice sentiment in theory, but it's not easily achievable for everyone to practice if their specific truth is something that has a history of being the object of people's hate and abuse, and continues to be a source of the same, even today. People still beat, murder, and degrade people who are different; every single day. A gay couple gets assaulted by a group of straight men when they exchange a kiss in public. A disabled teen is bullied at school because they are seen as easy targets because they don't have the verbal or physical ability to stand up for themselves. An adult who has severe depression is labeled as "crazy" and is treated as such at their job because they don't have the same ability as others to just go through life faking happiness.

The path to living one's truth is not an easy route for people and oftentimes when it's different from the majority of people around them, it can be seen as a threat. Even if only for the reason that it makes others confront their own fears, deficiencies, or stories. The unfortunate fact is that there are some who are so willing to do anything to preserve their sense of self and their truth, that they will choose to exert their belief in it even at the expense of someone else's humanity, and in some cases, someone else's life. This speaks to the power of people's stories and the life those stories are given when built by fear and hate.

Even with the risks that certain people groups may come up against when attempting to live fully in who they are, I've learned through my own experience that choosing to deny or suppress who you are, as a long term strategy, runs just as detrimental risks as sometimes putting yourself out there does. Now, I'm not suggesting that someone unwisely put themselves in harm's way in order to exert their individuality because you have to assess certain risks with wisdom and discernment. If you are in situations or environments on a regular basis where you're experiencing a real threat because of a differentiator, then you should use your best judgement to stay safe until you can leave that environment. If you are, however, in a generally and relatively safe environment to begin the journey of grounding your individual identity, then I hope and pray you will choose to come home to yourself. Allowing yourself to entangle your identity to any person or community of people, who would ever place being indistinguishable as a prerequisite to connection with them, will never be able to help you heal. That internal fracture will get worse and worse the more you try to cover up all that is inherently you. Even attempting to do so is almost as dangerous as looking to that same community of people to educate you on how to be something they absolutely are not. Whether you're Black, feeling fractured, yet looking to the white community to educate you on Black life, or if you're gay, feeling fractured, yet looking to your straight friends to help you identify better as a gay person, both are similar to wanting to be a doctor and yet going to a lawyer seeking education on how to perform surgeries.

Sure, they'll be able to rehash what they've learned from books, documentaries, podcasts, or their sister-in-law that's a doctor. They'll be able to recount the experiences they've had when they've had a surgery or tell you a story of a surgery their best friend in high school had. They may be able to give you regurgitated or rehearsed answers, but nothing they tell you will equip you to perform open-heart surgery. Even well-meaning guidance can set your life on the wrong course when you consider the source. This is why living as a fractured version of ourselves is so detrimental. It keeps us disconnected from the very people who can relate to us the most and can be pivotal in helping us connect to ourselves; because they may live a similar experience as you do every day. You need the love and support of both those who have different experiences from you as well as those who have similar experiences as you are on this journey of deep work if you want to both be whole and experience the world as a whole.

Part of being Black means you have to choose which is more important to you: approval or acknowledgment. The two are not synonymous. Approval tells you that you are good enough, only based on someone else's interpretation of what "good" looks like. Acknowledgement tells you that being you is all you need to be good enough. One is rooted in perception and the other is rooted in personhood. Part of being someone who wants to be an ally of the Black community requires you to audit your life and ask yourself if you've only been tolerant of Black people. Have you only been accepting of those who make you feel comfortable, or are you acknowledging them as whole, apart from your comfort zone and personal experience in this world? This is work that has to be an inside job. Being an ally isn't like getting the flu, where you can just catch inclusion by being around other people different from you. Creating space in your life for diverse relationships is a small part of it but the rest takes actionable steps and personal investment into being the bridge. No one can do it for you and no one should because we place more value into the things we have to work to earn.

It's no longer enough to have that one Black friend you go to for all your Black education and then use them as a personal reference on your "See, I like Black people" resume. It's not enough anymore to hide behind having a Black significant other as a way to say you couldn't possibly have any prejudices. It's not even enough to use the Black people that you may have in your family as a shield to hide behind when your privilege is being challenged. Having any of these things does not mean you're incapable of practicing racism or being discriminatory. It just means your specific form of prejudice is selective, that's all, but the prejudice can still be there and if it's still there, it will eventually show up even toward the people you've made an exception for. This is why it's no longer good enough for any of us to stop at the acceptance of one another. We all have to do better. Being born into this world is the only prerequisite for being accepted, which makes it the laziest attempt at healing this racial divide or at being a good human to others in general. We have to do better.

Before I really began to come home to myself as a Black woman, the level to which I censored myself was at an all-time high and it was constant. I would only display the humorous side of being Black with certain people because when I spoke about my experiences growing up and how parents of white friends were anything but welcoming to me when I came to their homes, it was too close for comfort for some people. There was a limit to my ability to express anything other than contentment, because getting upset made me "ghetto" when I was just trying to be heard like anyone else. I remember one time at a church potluck, someone had brought watermelon and as I was eating some a white church member made a passive aggressive comment about making sure I don't eat all the watermelon because they know how much Black people like watermelon. I felt so self-conscious about it that I never ate watermelon at a church function again. In fact, I was hyper aware of eating watermelon in front of anyone other than close family and friends after that. I get that this might sound ridiculous to some people, that I stopped eating watermelon because of a weird micro aggressive comment. But this is just one example of how some comments made about a person's race, ethnicity, culture, or any other distinctive trait has the potential to end up becoming weapons that assassinate someone's sense of self. The "You're so pretty for a Black girl" when you're trying to date and the "Maybe you'd make more sales if you acted like one of them - you know - so they could trust you", when you're in the workplace, chip away at minorities every day. These seemingly small but impactful interactions reinforce what most minorities already know, which is that our kind of difference is often looked at as something that needs a workaround. So often our experience has included being required to be a reflection of normalcy so when people look at us, they're never faced with having to work at understanding what it is they are seeing.

I remember how, through the years, this reality showed up in my life when I began talking about me being a Black woman and some of the experiences I've had being discriminated against because of it. I was having these conversations as a way to help the person I was talking to understand that racism is still an active part of our society, and I would get the response "I mean yeah, you're Black, but you're not BLACK BLACK. You're practically a white girl in a Black girl's body". THAT was their response. No questions. No curiosity about what I was trying to say. Just a rebuttal to me sharing my Black experience. I got this response so often when trying to share the realities of being different. Honestly, for years I would just laugh it off and then quickly shift the conversation to something light because I immediately let that comment intimidate me into believing that my Black experience wasn't Black enough to be valid. It was as if they said "Sure you're Black enough for us to see that you're different, but not Black enough to where you could possibly make anyone feel uncomfortable. You're much more like us than other Black people". It's extremely discouraging to feel as if you can't even keep ownership of your own story. It's like, dang, what parts of me can I keep and still be seen as me? The funny thing is that as time went on, and the more I identified with my Blackness, the more others began to identify it and all of a sudden, things started to shift. For some, I wasn't as welcomed with open arms as I was before. The comfort they once felt with me started to fade, and I soon became just another Black person to them. I was no longer the exception because I stepped out of character and I was no longer molding myself into whatever version of Black that would most properly fit the space I was in. For others, my experiences as a Black woman were being taken more seriously than before. I was being seen and experienced, maybe not fully just yet, but definitely more authentically than before. The happier I was with being Black, the more I celebrated it and loved it, the more the people who loved me wanted to join in on the celebration too. I realized how I had done a great disservice to everyone, including myself, by allowing a co-dependent relationship between myself and the white community to go on for so long. One where I was dependent on their validation and where some of them were dependent on me to be a cardboard cutout version of Black representation in their life. I did a disservice to my friendships by not interacting with them authentically and allowing them to love me completely. The gig was up. I couldn't have kept it going even if I had wanted to. Once the veil is lifted from your eyes about inequality and you no longer see things through rose colored glasses, but you see things as they truly are, ignorance is no longer bliss. It's a prison cell that you can't stand the idea of going back into.

I began to recognize all of the microaggressions that were thrown at me on a daily basis that I always just passed off as sarcasm. I saw all the double standards and inconsistencies amongst how certain people were treated as opposed to others and I could no longer just pass it all off by saying "Well we're only human". I could no longer overlook the ways the elderly addressed me and treated me just because "They come from a different generation". I could no longer give excuses for why someone I was close to and was so kind to me, would also make comments about Black people such as "It's unfortunate that most Black people just don't work hard enough to make something of themselves. If they would just get out of their ghetto mentality then there would be more successful Black people in the world". These things I could no longer turn a deaf ear to. I recognized that if I was to be the only Black experience someone might have in real life, then I was going to make it count. The moment I chose not to take the opportunity to use my voice when statements like those left someone's lips, is the moment I chose to make an active contribution to ignorance. I could no longer just excuse it by saying "Well they don't know any better" when I could have shared something better.

Even now I can't help but cringe as I recount the years of my light privilege, the ways I suppressed my Blackness and relied on the white community to define it for me, and the ways that I kept quiet when I should have used my voice. I wish that I had grown into myself much earlier in life and that I had a more in-depth view of the diversity of Blackness as well as the diversity of racism earlier on, but I didn't because I was not experiencing one and I was participating in the other. This is why this book was never going to be just one thing. It was never going to be a book that only spoke to Black people or only spoke to white people. It was never going to be a book that only spoke about racism or only spoke about survival. It was never meant to be one thing, just as none of us were meant to be one thing. I speak on racism and prejudice because I have been both a perpetrator of them as well as a recipient. I speak about Blackness as someone who has been both disconnected from it and has had my own experience of it. My story has afforded me the opportunity to have a dual perspective that can be tough for some to hear, hard for others to accept, and sure as heck has not been easy for me to live. Even though it has been a journey in which I felt divided within myself so often, it's still a part of my story and the turbulence of it has been part of the platform that I'm able to speak from today. It's a journey that is still happening because this is what the path of being a lifelong learner looks like. You never camp out anywhere for very long because there's always more to be discovered.

My hope is that someone reading this book may find comfort in knowing that they are not alone, that their greatest strength while trying to learn how to be themselves in the world is their vulnerability, and that they deserve a life in which they can live it as a whole person regardless of what parts of them other people are willing to accept or not accept.

If you are that person, I hope you will settle for nothing less.

SIX - The Other Side of Hurt

Have you ever heard the saying "Hurting people, hurt people"? I first heard it when listening to author and speaker Joyce Meyer say it in one of her television appearances. Essentially, it is the belief that if you have suffered hurt, and do not seek out the healing and wholeness you need in order to prevent that hurt from consuming you, then you will perpetuate the same or similar hurt onto someone else. Then, if that person doesn't heal from the hurt you perpetuated onto them, they will do the same to someone else, and the cycle goes on and on. Hurting people hurt people, that hurt people, that hurt people, that hurt people.

This is true of any and every hurt, torment, and pain inflicted on humans today. It is true of abuse, of sexual assault, of bullying, and it is profoundly true of racism. This is essentially how racism is passed down from generation to generation. It is essentially how racism has spread like a virus through the blood of our nation. It is how so many white people have lived in fear of the Black community and the Black community has lived in suspicion of white people. The unhealed, unchecked wounds of both parties end up creating a cycle of hurt for themselves, their communities, their families, and one another. Like wealth that can be handed down and inherited by way of a will, we can hand down biases, fear, and division through our shear will to not let go of what we've been taught. Our future generations inherit the hurt we've nurtured.

Right now in the world, we are in the midst of a pandemic of epic proportions. COVID-19 has ravaged our country, stolen our time, our health, our freedom, and for many it's stolen the lives of their family and friends. Paralleling these unprecedented times is a social upheaval that has proven to be brewing under the perfect conditions for a revolution. We've got the recorded murder of George Floyd by the hands of law enforcement that knelt on his neck after him telling them, repeatedly, that he couldn't breathe. There's the gunning down of Ahmaud Arbery while he was on a jog that happened in the earlier part of 2020 but was only brought to light after a recording of it was shared. All the while, the murder was covered up and his murderers were not brought to justice. Breonna Taylor was shot and killed during a questionable police raid. These are just recent accounts that have made headlines, but this stuff is happening every day and has been for decades. The murder of Black men and women is not new news to the Black community. Fear of retaliation or harsher punishments than necessary as a consequence of the color of your skin is nothing new to us. Wondering if local authorities are going to single you out when you're minding your own business walking down the street is for many just a factor of their everyday life. The face of racism and how loudly it speaks has ebbed and flowed over the years. Some would say it's gotten better. Others would disagree. I would say that it's just gotten smarter and those bleeding it out into the world have gotten more stealthy. It's never not been here though. It's just been more of an undercurrent than a wave.

If you have recounted history and how this country was literally built on the backs of Black people, and if you have witnessed the injustices and brutality prevalent in our society today, I cannot imagine for a second that anyone would tell Black people that we do not have a reason to be angry. That we don't have a reason to be frustrated, afraid, and skeptical of any partnerships formed with those in the white community. Yet, as inconceivable as it is to me that there would be those who deny the stark evidence of brutality, racism, and bias, the reality is that there are still so many in denial of it. There are still so many who choose to deny the Black community the history we have come from, the loss of life that has been as a result of historical and modern-day lynching's, the public displays of racism that are just a Google search or FB comment away. They choose to discredit an entire people group and the lives of every civil rights leader our country has ever known.

I wonder though, for those who choose to discredit the history of Black people based on one's need to feel they should be absolved of any responsibility for the healing of the current divide, then does that mean all white history connected to Black history is also discredited? White history created slavery. Slaves didn't bring themselves to the United States and say "Gee, we feel that our main purpose in life is to serve white people, be denied basic human privileges, be separated from our families, raped, beaten, and treated like cattle to be sold!" No, they were brought here against their will for the purpose of enslavement, it was decided for them what and who they would be here in America and the rest was, well, history. Slavery was intentionally created, and systems were strategically put in place to keep slaves in their place for a very long time. Yes, I know YOU didn't specifically create slavery, but the privilege that has always been present as a shared experience for all white people has most certainly played a role in giving life to it and to the current symptoms of its history in this country.

Since slavery didn't just happen like the Big Bang theory, I have a few questions for those who want to discredit Black history, and who might want to discredit the Black experience. When you consider that slavery was created and facilitated by white people, how do you separate two histories that are so tightly woven together? How can you rightly acknowledge the existence of one without the other? Who and what created slavery in the United States? What was one of the driving forces behind creating law enforcement, who created it, and what kind of people were they trying to enforce laws over? Who created segregation, felt the need to have separate bathrooms, drinking fountains, and would assault or murder any Black person who tried to buck that system? These are questions that I challenge you to ask yourself if you feel the temptation to discredit the persecution that the Black community has suffered for generations. The history of subhuman treatment didn't stop when politically supported segregation ended. When you consider the fact that people, given strength by their shared hatred, have continued to create their own legal systems in which they are the judge, jury, and executioner in communities across the nation, even in current times. We, the Black community, has suffered great hurt. We share in the hurt of our ancestors, we share in the hurt of Black people who are suffering at the hands of injustice today, and we continue to experience our own hurts in our own lives. This is the truth of many Black lives today.

If you're reading this book as someone not a part of the Black community, one who is seeking understanding, wanting to come into partnership with us to close this racial divide, I believe it is possible you have experienced some kind of hurt as well. Especially if you are trying to be a part of creating a level playing field for Black people, or even if you're just curious, I want you to know that I see you. You may have experienced the hurt that can be felt through empathy, the hurt that can be felt when someone close to you, who's Black, recounts the racism and discrimination they've experienced. It could be hurt you feel when you see videos of police brutality, or it could even be hurt that you've experienced because you feel mistaken for a collaborator of racism when you are very much an opposer of it. Though your hurt may not be the same kind of hurt that the Black community has experienced, to me hurt is not a competition and scars still form no matter what created them. The only difference is that some are closer to the surface and fade a little over time, while others are from deep wounds that leave deep marks.

I've felt the hurt of those who share the weight of the injustice that Black people have suffered, yet feel as if they don't know how to be a part of the healing process. I've seen the tears of those who have wept for the lost lives of Black people due to police brutality. I have heard the cries for peace from the mouths of our allies and people who care about us. The hurt may be different because of the difference in our experiences, but we are all hurting. In no way would I ever say that other communities are not joining us in our sadness, fear, and anger, because that is just not true. To say that others couldn't possibly partner with us in the pain would be denying the existence of many loving people who want to see our modern-day emancipation as much as we do.

I have both been hurt and I have witnessed hurt. I have witnessed a hurt that I could have easily been a perpetrator of, if I allowed myself to. That is the hurt caused by the shame some of us in the Black community have rained down on those who are white, just for being white, even if they are allies and not agents of hate. I have witnessed the humiliation some have imposed on those who don't know, what they don't know, because they haven't had the Black experience that we have. In some cases, the blatant bullying is directed at those who try to engage in a conversation with us about being Black. Yes, there are those that say extremely ignorant things that can elicit frustration and anger, but the actual definition of ignorance is simply the state of not having knowledge or education about something. That's all. Being ignorant is not always synonymous with being apathetic or not caring and I think there are times we internalize ignorance and criticize it too harshly. It's as if when a person says, "I wasn't aware of that" it is being translated as, "I don't care about that". This is not always the case.

Yes, there are people who say incredibly ridiculous things

in order to start a debate without the goal of coming to an understanding, instead wanting to argue just for the sake of arguing. Yes, there are people who are rude because they know just what to say to press your buttons and they enjoy being able to say they encountered yet another angry Black person. Yes, there are even things people say that make you roll your eyes, laugh an exasperated laugh, then wonder how it is that they have survived life thus far! On the flipside of this, it's important to remember that just as no Black person is the voice for all Black people, so it is that no one else can speak for their entire community either. The ignorance of one person shouldn't be taken as the ignorance of all. With racism and prejudice being on such a grand scale, I understand how easy it is to judge the whole by the individual encounters you've had. I'm also empathetic to how easy it is to be influenced by the stories you've heard from people close to you, or by the things you see on TV. However, isn't that how Black people get lumped into one big "They're all ghetto, they're all mad, they're all violent, they're all uneducated" generalized group in which none of us are looked at as unique or diverse?

Uh huh.

That's me calling the kettle black. No pun intended.

I'm a Black woman who has become used to being the primary source of Black information to the primarily white community that I've been a part of all my life. I've fielded too many questions to recount. Some easy, some difficult and intimate, and many where I just wanted to respond with a downward glance, while I shake my head, rub my temples and say "I just can't with you right now". Trust me, I get it. Though

I would repeatedly find myself in situations where I was looked at as having all the answers and like I was THE BLACK VOICE, as long as the conversation was a healthy exchange, I chose to lean into it. I didn't shy away. I didn't allow my internal dialogue of "*I cannot believe she just asked me if Black people could grow hair! What kind of stupid question is that?*" determine how much grace I allotted them. I just showed up and took the opportunity I was presented with to tell my story and be part of creating space for someone to consider something other than what they've previously thought. In the process of doing that I found that I would often walk away considering something other than what I previously thought too.

The honest reality is that, more often than not, when I bring up the concept of the Black community being more open to having these kinds of conversations, the reaction that I typically get is something along the lines of "I am so tired of educating white people though! Like, in this day and age where you can find out anything, they should know these things by now. If they don't know then I just feel like it's because they don't care. The information is available if they really want it." I mean, you ain't wrong! The information is readily available for anyone who wants it. There are podcasts, audiobooks, and TED talks that go deep into providing insight from a diverse array of people and stories. The information isn't hiding, it just needs to be sought after. The questions I can't help but ponder though is "But why don't we consider the action they have taken by coming to the source of Black life, those in the Black community, as a part of them taking initiative? Why does that not count for anything? Am I missing something here?" If the Black community wants to hold the white community accountable for taking the initiative to become aware, then I guess I just wonder what we expect the internet to teach them that we can't when they're right in front of us? Sure, they could get information online or in a book, but we have the opportunity to offer real accounts in a personable way that creates space for a 2-way dialogue. Instead, some of us would rather send them out into a world that doesn't always understand us itself, and doesn't come with the power of our personal stories told with our unique voice.

Where is the line between not wanting to have someone depend on us for their primary education and us just choosing not to give of our time? So please, indulge me a moment, because I have a thought. What if we started to consider the idea that we are the experts in the matter of the diversity of Blackness? That we are the Black professionals of life. I wonder if we might then have an internal shift when it comes to how we perceive the white community asking us questions even when they may seem like ignorant ones and we just don't feel like engaging? Just stay with me a moment while I walk you through what I mean.

Being an expert is a form of leadership. If you work in a company where people consider you an expert at your job, you are considered a leader because people understand that they can trust what you have to say, because you have a level of expertise they do not have. That's why they come to YOU when they don't understand why something isn't working. That's why they come to YOU when the numbers aren't adding up. It's because YOU are the expert and they know that when no one else knows what's going on, you are a reliable source. Any time someone is looking to you for guidance, answers, or insight, there is a role shift that happens, sometimes, ever so slightly that it's not even easy to recognize it. In that moment, when you have the answer, you are leading them. When utilizing your leadership role, you could end up helping to shape the way they see and interact with the world when they walk away from that conversation with you. What an awesome opportunity you've been given! Whether the question seems silly, you're tired of answering questions, or you want to just brush them off and tell them to "Google it", if someone presents you with questions, there is a role shift that happens. You, as the expert, are momentarily passed the baton to lead. They, possibly without even knowing it, have submitted their lack of understanding just enough to have the very act of asking be a confession that they may not know it all. The simple act of asking questions is a form of submission. Whether they stay open or not, once the conversation begins and ends is obviously out of your control. But I wonder how our inner narrative might sound differently if we look at questions as an invitation for leadership instead of an inconvenience?

I myself have been the target of what I would consider a verbal vomiting of questions thrown up at me like rapid fire from people, and I too have fantasized about just throwing my hands up and 'peace the heck out' of there. So, I'm by no means saying there is no cause for annoyance. Sometimes you just want to live your life. You just want to be able to enjoy dinner with friends just like anyone else. You want to be able to visit someone's church and experience the typical meet-

and-greet that always happens when a new person walks in. You want to be able to make a new business connection without having the spotlight be on the fact that you're Black, which is nothing new to you! I've been there and done that, believe me. Maybe it's my personality, the way God wired me, or the way my particular experiences shaped the way I see the world (most likely the answer is a combination of all three). But I just found myself feeling frustrated more often than not when watching how some within the Black community responded to white people who ask them questions about anything pertaining to being Black. I was frustrated with how I've witnessed some be indignant about how white people don't understand us, how they don't care about us, how they judge us without knowing us. Then, when a white person, in one way or another, asks questions to try to get an understanding our response is hostility toward them for not already knowing the answer. There'd be a response of irritation that they're asking the question in the first place, or a "See, that statement right there proves that you don't have a clue about Black people!" And then it would almost seem like the only option in that moment would be for someone to walk away because the bridge was already on fire at that point. I've seen the aftermath of a white person being left to sit with all the anger and annoyance that was thrown at them and after all that, they left that conversation just as ignorant as they came. Only now, on top of their ignorance, they are bewildered, mad, offended, embarrassed, defensive, and the probability that they will ever engage in a conversation about race with any Black person again is slim because they still feel the sting from their last attempt.

In my life throughout the years these scenes would evolve and they'd involve different characters, but the endings were too often very similar. I've seen them when I was young and in school, I've seen it in the workplace, with family members, in the church, and just out observing the community I lived in. A non-antagonizing white person would say something about Black people that clearly showed they didn't know what they were talking about, and the Black person or people in earshot would go off on this person. They would rain holy hell on them until this person cried, until they caved under the pressure and lashed out, or until they just imploded silently. Again, the result is that they walked away not fully understanding the exchange, why what they said may have been perceived as offensive (in some of these cases why it was that the other person became defensive from the start), and the ONLY impression that is left on them is the tongue lashing they received. There was no discussion. There was no exchange of information. No enlightenment. No resolve. No common ground. No opportunity for either party to learn anything from the other. There was no invitation to explore or be curious as to why someone thought what they said wasn't correct or appropriate. NOTHING. Not even an opportunity to agree to disagree. The only result was that one party walked away feeling justified in their annoyance and the other walked away confused as another nail was hammered into the coffin of their Black assumptions.

Don't misunderstand me here. It is still NOT the Black community's responsibility to be a warm glass of milk for people, in order to help them feel comfortable with the responses to their questions or remarks. The reality is that those who are Black are required in one-way shape or form to suppress large parts of themselves on a daily basis if their lives are deeply intertwined with the white community. We are required to suppress our Blackness in a plethora of ways that can often make it hard to ever be in a state of transparency, authenticity, and ease within our own day-to-day lives outside the comfort of our own homes. This is something that many who aren't people of color may not take into consideration about our experiences in America. I mean, why would they? If the vast majority of people that you are surrounded by in your life look familiar because they have a similar skin tone as you, have similar family structures, and create community in a way similar to the way you do, you are usually not going to have the day-to-day task of having to tailor how you show up in the world. You're not concerned with softening the blow of all the assumptions that will be made about you, based on factors you cannot control and are identifiable by anyone in view of you. To have to intellectually consider how to interact with people in a way that doesn't draw attention to the fact that not only does your experience of the world look very different from others, but to live with the understanding that one reason your experience is so different is because of the dynamics of being a minority in a majority population that still has a sense of hostility toward your community today. Honestly, it can be exhausting and if you're not careful you can end up suppressing who you are so deeply, that you begin to lose touch with it all together, or you run the risk of living your life in the shadow of resentment.

Now some of you may be wondering what I'm trying to get at. What's the point of all of it? You may be thinking that

I'm surely going to connect the dots and come to some kind of conclusion that says white people are the problem, or that Black people are the problem because someone here has got to be the one we can point a finger at and say, "See! This is why we can't be friends!" Well, I hate to break it to you but if that's what you're hoping for - I'm not going to be able to meet your expectations. I say that not because I don't have an opinion or because I find it thrilling to be vague. I say all of this to spark thought. To inspire you to be curious about yourself and the person opposite you. To challenge the Black community's perception of what it means to be a source of Black understanding for the white community and to challenge the white community's sense of ownership over the Black experience even while engaging in the act of trying to understand it.

As Black people, our experiences are our own and what experiences we share, we do so out of choice - not because we are a vending machine for Black information in which one can expect to get something to nibble on every time you put a dollar in it. Snacks don't make up a meal and a full-scale Black inquisition on someone you personally know, or just met, shouldn't fully replace your own effort to educate yourself. The story of Black lives as told by Black people in real life should be a supplement to all that you already have intentionally tried to learn on your own, so don't overlook your own ability to come to the table with something too! Come with something we can confirm, or back up, or engage in a mutual discussion about, instead of presenting as an empty bucket, hoping we will have all the water you need to fill your well. To my Black peeps, lean into moments of leadership. Step into the expertise that only you have and don't be afraid to be understood. There is a gift in retelling the story of who you are and why you are, it's that you always stay grounded in that knowing - even when the world tells you that your kind of Blackness is too loud, too bold, too obvious, too bland, or too whatever. Let's both come to the table with a plate to share. Doing so will ensure that we all leave the table full.

SEVEN - Say Their Names

I'm sitting in my room writing this book and marveling at the fact that I am living in a time where our nation is experiencing a boiling pot of emotions and experiences. The tension in the air is so thick you can cut it with a knife. There is so much tangible anger that has been stirred up in communities across the United States, and the world, since the death of George Floyd. His death was both a tragedy and a catalyst for change that Black people and the nation needed. It was the springboard that gave activism and anti-racism in our present day, more momentum and elevated their platforms. The impact that his death has had on every single person, whether they are for Black lives or not, is the thing that history will be made of. I am living in the middle of a deeply impactful historical moment that will be spoken about for generations. The names of Black people that have died as a result of negligence, police brutality, and unadulterated racism, will never leave the lips of this nation.

As I tear up right now, I can't help but wonder what these victims' lives were filled with? I wonder what they thought about before they went to bed every night or what first came to mind when they woke up every morning. We have been caught in the riptide of the change their deaths have inspired but did they live their life feeling inspired by their existence? Did Breonna Taylor ever imagine leading her community into a revolution? Did Ahmaud Arbery ever become overwhelmed with frustration that he wasn't being heard? Did they ever feel this deep leading to step out and challenge the status quo, but then decided to stay back because they didn't know how they could actually make a difference? Did George Floyd ever imagine that his daughter Gianna's words of "Daddy changed the world," would actually play a role in changing the world? There was a purpose that became of their deaths because Black people have had enough of seeing Black bodies hit the ground to never come back up again. We didn't just see Ahmaud, Breonna, George, and the countless others that died before them due to an abuse of power or racism. We looked into their eyes and saw our own staring back at us because history has shown that to many, the disposability of one Black life is a reflection of how easily disposable all Black lives are.

It goes without saying that so often a person gets much due recognition, love, and admiration in death in a way that they should have gotten in life. If you've ever loved someone and then lost them, I would guess you know what it feels like to get a new perspective in their death that made you wish you would have loved them more, or paid them more attention in life. When I think of my Grandma who passed away, I think and speak of her fondly. I talk about how much she loved me and how much fun we would have dancing together, and about the times she skated with me at the roller rink when I was younger. And how all my friends were jealous that I had such a cool Grandma who could out jam skate any of us. Her death casts the colors of a beautiful summer sunset over her life when I think about her now. She was my rock that I didn't even realize I had. Yet when I look at her life under a microscope instead of through rose-colored glasses, I see a truth that I still find myself grappling with. The truth of days passed that I didn't call and didn't visit. The nights passed where she came to mind but I didn't take a moment to say a prayer for her. When we think back on the lives of those we've lost, these secret places create moments of reflection and they make you wonder. If you love them this passionately now, even though you didn't give them as much as you could have, how much deeper could your relationship have been if you had loved them this hard in life too? It's an interesting paradigm and it makes me wonder how much more impactful all of our lives could be if we reverse engineered our legacy? If we lived out loud right now the legacy we want to leave later? In what ways might we be walking through life postponing the impact we could have today for a day that will carry our memory but not the power that could come from our presence?

Protesting is currently one of the most prevalent forms of activism being participated in right now and it's such a beautiful thing. So many in the Black community are returning back to the activist roots of many who went before us, paving a way for our future. I know I feel that connection! Through my own protesting I found out that my Grandma left her kids with my Grandpa, got on a bus with people from work, and traveled from Holland, Michigan to Washington DC to the

March on Washington that Martin Luther King Jr. was at, which was something that either I didn't previously know about or I had forgotten. Though I wasn't marching in front of the White House like she did, I was still marching, and there was something about the knowledge of our shared experiences that made me feel so proud to be her Granddaughter. It was a very surprising link to a part of my family's story that I wasn't even looking to find. It also really brought to life for me how our advocacy for Black lives not only supports our present and builds our future, but it also gives validation to the past. I don't know about you, but I want the hard work that my family members and ancestors put in to give us our freedom to be validated.

Amidst the protesting, there has been a tremendous amount of rioting accompanying them. There are peaceful protests that start out as intended and then transform into something the organizers never intended them to be, and with every large movement it is to be expected that there will be imposters that ride the coattails of a well-meaning message and the fight for Black lives is not excluded from this. However, it quickly became clear that the purpose behind the protests was beginning to get overshadowed by what looked like retaliation dressed in the costume of good intentions. The downtowns of many cities have experienced fires, vandalism, looting, and the otherwise bustling streets of a thriving community have been turned into a scene from The Purge making some wonder what exactly went wrong. Yes, we had people posing as those in support of Black lives that would piggyback off of peaceful protests but were really just anarchists, more interested in raging against authority in general and had very little interest in supporting Black lives. Yet the protests and protesters are what got blamed for everything that went wrong. You had racists and others with ill intent causing destruction knowing full well that the protesters and the Black community would be blamed for it - which they often did. You had people from the Black community, who were a part of destroying storefronts and those so angry and frustrated they took it out on brick and glass instead of flesh and bone.

It's been hard to watch for so many reasons. It's been hard to watch because it may be the town you love and enjoy that you've watched being vandalized. It's hard to watch because maybe you were a store owner that built a restaurant from the ground up that's now in shambles. It's been hard because maybe you struggle to feel connected to a community that you think may have been a part of destroying itself. Maybe it's even hard to watch because you have supported a movement that now makes you feel torn between commitment to community and commitment to a mission. I myself have even wondered at times when I'd watch footage of riots happening all over the nation "How did we get here and how do we trace our steps back to where we started?" Even when you knew that the rioting was not necessarily synonymous with the protesting, it still felt so heavy, so surreal, and wildly unimaginable. Outside of those who were looking to take advantage of social change platforms, I viewed the rioting as a form of protesting for some who may have experienced a torment that words alone and holding a sign saying "Being Black is not a crime" could not come close to expressing. As a Black woman who has admittedly experienced my own privilege, I know without a doubt that there are ways Black people are being chastised by the police, by other authorities, by religious leaders, by teachers, by sales associates, gas station clerks, by waiters, and by the stranger sitting a couple seats away from them on the train, that chip away at you day after day. Each trauma causes a little fire here and a little fire there until there are so many little fires burning that it's as if the insides of a person are completely engulfed.

This is where the anger of so many comes from. They are experiencing the fires within that are being stoked each day that Breonna Taylor didn't get justice. They're stoked every time we read the comment section of an online post covering a protest where people make bold statements from behind a screen and they are stoked every time they experience blatant discrimination. These fires are as real as what started them.

In our pursuit for justice and as we work through the kaleidoscope of feelings that we're experiencing, I believe it's so important that we strive to source our momentum from the mission, not solely from passion. We must make it a practice to check in with ourselves to make sure we do not become addicted to our anger. That we do not source all of our momentum from fury and end up taking away from the mission what should be added to it. We must protect our minds and hearts from creating a drug out of anger, then getting so addicted that we are looking for our next fix around every corner. You'll know you're addicted to anger when you seek out media coverage, posts and comments, and you become an instigator in certain kinds of conversations to trigger your anger. Anger, as a drug, is deceptive in that when you get that hit, you may feel like you are ready to take on anything. But the trick is that you have to keep feeding that anger in order to keep your trajectory. So, you seek out a hit of anger, you ride it out and let it energize you until it starts to die down, then you seek out something more to stoke the flames again. This can keep repeating for as long as your determination to stay angry exists.

Even when anger is justified, the perpetuation of this cycle doesn't aid in the mission of justice for people of color, instead it distracts from it. You may be thinking "No, it doesn't distract from the mission! I'm angry ABOUT injustice. I'm angry ABOUT police brutality. I'm angry ABOUT inequality. My anger has a focus." Well, I don't doubt that your anger has a focus, but the focus in and of itself isn't what brings about change. I believe it's the way in which you choose to focus that will play a pivotal role in guiding your actions to spark real change. I mean, I can focus on a salad all day long, but if I don't eat it then it sure isn't going to do anything for me now is it? I can focus on that salad and think about how much I hate salads, how I'd rather be eating french fries, and how every salad I've ever eaten I've hated. More than likely the result will be that the salad will in no way touch my lips. I could also focus on how I'm not a fan of them, but that eating them will improve my health so I can have a better quality of life, I'll have more energy during the day, and better rest at night. That kind of focus can shift my energy to something that will be beneficial. We have so many valid reasons to be angry, to want to scream, to cry, to yell, and to punch a wall, but the power isn't in the punch...it's in the purpose.

Almost immediately following the stories of vandalism during or after protests, people were so upset about the destruction of property, that they started to gloss over the reason there was such chaos in the first place. Why there was rioting in the first place! I watched the headlines online and heard conversation start to shift away from police brutality, away from George Floyd, away from the murders that were a direct result of racism, and very quickly all some could see were the flames engulfing people instead of focusing on what it was that set them on fire to begin with. Those who chose to distract from the movement, those who desired a change of subject, those who wanted to have a reason to say that protesting doesn't have value anymore, and those who couldn't wait to discredit the Black community and our allies almost won. Almost.

I remember observing this shift in focus and how the shift in outrage over brutality evolved into outrage over the windows of our favorite restaurant being busted out and somehow the attention span held for an inanimate object seemed to have more resolve than the fair-weather allegiance these same people pledged to the cause just a few weeks ago. I witnessed the gradual decline in public displays of support by some, once things started to get intense. I recognized the flinches from people when they'd see the Black power fist and how it was now being viewed as if it was akin to the middle finger instead of the gesture of solidarity that it represents so much today. I heard how the shouts of "Black lives matter!" begin to die down as if by saying it you were now labeling yourself as an anti-white, anti-humanitarian, anti-American terrorist. I feared the dissolution of one of the most important racial justice movements of my generation and was concerned that it would begin to be thrown out the window because many were too caught up in, "How dare they do this to our city!" Currently there still is some of this sentiment lingering in the air. The only difference is that from the start of the protesting just a couple of months ago to now, there have been more deaths due to police brutality, more injustices, and more video evidence. It only continues to substantiate the 'why' behind the need for reform in this country. I keep thinking that, if at this point there are still people who continue to make the damages that have come as a result of some of the protesting and rioting the main object of contention, then they are a living breathing example of why over 150 years after slavery was abolished in the United States, Black people are still being treated like being Black is a crime against humanity.

Thankfully because of the awareness, the call to action, and the call to accountability that has been brought about by the nationwide collective efforts of the Black community and our allies, there has been measurable progress made for the rights and protection of Black people! New policies are being created to bring more accountability to law enforcement like "Breonna's Law" which was passed in Louisville after the death of Breonna Taylor, which bans no-knock warrants. There are questionable law enforcement officers who are being let go or resigning from their positions. There are more and more police brutality recordings being made and shared, and because of mounting pressure, some of these same police are being almost immediately fired or suspended. Monuments that have celebrated confederates have been removed in some states. People from all over the world have been fighting and protesting for the lives of Black people everywhere. Those who have scoffed at protesters, have said they're wasting time, that protesting is outdated and isn't the way to change, many of them have now started to eat their words. There has been great change and greater change continues to be had.

There is power in numbers. I think we all know that innately. We recognize this when one of our friends or family members is getting bullied and we rally with them to intimidate the aggressor. Numbers are what give momentum to the influence of religion and philosophies, and numbers are the driving force behind if you are considered a social media "influencer" or not. There's power in numbers. Which is why I just can't figure out why it is, that so often it takes some kind of insurmountable pressure to inspire us all to finally combine our wills, come together, and create the support system we've been waiting for someone else to provide? Why does it take Black people literally dying in the streets, unnecessarily being shot in their homes, or the evidence of a white woman in a park falsely accusing a Black man of assault on a recorded video to finally say "You know what, there are a lot of US and there are also many WITH US. Maybe we should come out of our homes and attack this thing head on together? Maybe?" I mean, I just don't get why things need to get to this level before linking arms with one another? Why are these nationwide protests such a phenomena when it should have always been the standard? Our lack of rights, our suppressed lives, our deaths, our abuse, our tears, our hurt, has always been the standard from the moment African people were kidnapped from their homes and brought here with the sole intent of being house pets that work the fields and do the laundry.

I'm frustrated. I'm sad. I'm overwhelmed. It's no new news to many of us that facets of Black life have always mattered to some within the white community. Our hair has mattered. Our music mattered. It mattered whether our brown or black skin was able to get sunburned or not. The curves of our body have always mattered. To others in the white community our rights, our justice, and our equality has also mattered. Yet what I feel we need right now, just as much as knowing our lives matter in general, is to feel like our lives matter to other Black people as well. To feel like our voice bears weight in the life of a Black person who lives differently from us without feeling like we can only speak into the lives of those whose Blackness is only akin to our own. What I personally needed most was to step outside of my bubble and reach out my hand to clasp the hand next to me. That is part of what fills me up right now even in the midst of these heartbreaking times and I think there are others who can relate to this celebration of reunification within the Black community. So many of us have lived segregated from one another for far too long, either by choice or circumstance. In many ways it felt like we had forgotten the comradery that I believe many of our ancestors understood, but that we had become disconnected from over the years. Partially due to the little technological comfort bubbles that we live in every time we escape to our phones instead of lifting our eyes to meet those of the other person we pass on the street. Sometimes I even feel like we almost forgot that Black life has always mattered. I'm not talking about our lives as individuals but I'm talking about the Black lifeforce that ties us all together and that we now are beginning to recognize within one another. We are finally starting to see ourselves in each other's eyes again. It's time. It's time we rise to our feet, raise our heads, and look at the world and each other straight in the eye. It's time we not just look inward for our own strength but that we look side to side to celebrate the strength of the people next to us. It's time to reclaim the excitement of the pursuit of our wholeness as a community. Brothers, sisters, and allies: If we are to claim the full life that Black people have on this planet, that is equally and fully ours to have, then we have to shift our priorities. We have to shift our priorities from me, myself, and mine to us, to we, and ours.

EIGHT - It's an Inside Job

Protesting, challenging policies, requiring acknowledge-ment - not just acceptance, and unity, are just fractions of the work that needs to be done. Must haves in order to step into the fullness of the life we deserve on this planet, that is as fully ours, as it is fully anyone else's. To me, protesting, pushing for policy changes, demanding the acknowledgement that Black lives matter, and building community with one another is the easier part of this fight. Don't get me wrong, I'm not saying that the work it takes to accomplish these things doesn't require effort, because it most certainly does! I'm doing my part in so many ways, which includes writing this book. It takes a tremendous amount of time, effort, sleepless nights, and tears to put in the work required to inspire, challenge, and change the way the Black community is being treated. What I mean by the "easier part" of the fight is that it's often easier to project the need for change onto outside influences, than it is to champion for change within ourselves and within our own homes.

Have you ever been in a fight with someone and you're

trying to make a point about how something they did or said hurt you, and they come back at you with an example in which you did the exact same thing to them? I know I have! At that moment my knee jerk reaction is to be all, "Don't change the subject! We're talking about you right now, not me!" Please tell me I am not the only one who pulled the old we're-not-talking-about-me-right-now trick? This is an example of what I mean when I say protesting is the easier part. In some instances, protesting can be seen as a large-scale public argument about demanding our need to be heard. It is oftentimes easier to participate in because we wouldn't be there if we weren't already passionate about what we're speaking out about! However, what happens when the people on the receiving end of our demands, challenge us by bringing up OUR role in the argument? What then? Will we choose to deflect and say "We're not talking about me right now"? What happens if we deflect in this way and defer our introspection for another time that feels better to us? I believe that it's possible we may be robbing ourselves of a valuable opportunity for growth if we deflect and defer. We may miss out on getting a deeper understanding of why we feel what we feel. We might even end up robbing ourselves of the opportunity for real change instead of what can sometimes translate into passionate venting with very little idea of what we want to walk away from the interaction with. Is it possible that there are additional efforts that should be made that have nothing to do with anyone else, but everything to do with the stories we tell ourselves?

This is where I believe some of the hardest work comes in and also where some of the greatest progress begins. Once we have all the rights we are fighting for, once we have the equal treatment for all humans that we're demanding, once we are heard, and once we are seen, then what? Once we no longer have the constant presence of someone else on the receiving end of our demands, then what is left? Well, what is left - is us. What is left is only new growth now that we've gotten to the very baseline of what should have been the entire time. This is hard to conceptualize, I know. The idea of a more unified world in which we don't just pick and choose which parts of a community benefit us, like the love for Latin food but the maltreatment of Latin people; or listening to Black music but hatred of Black people, can seem like a lofty goal. But you cannot confidently head toward a destination you don't believe exists. We have to keep the highest level of equality leading the way we interact with the world, which is no easy feat and will not be without missteps. Ultimately, this is when the deep work of creating our new normal begins and living out old divisive patterns end; and there's no better time to begin this work than right now. There are no perfect conditions in which it will be easier to challenge our intentions or push ourselves to prioritize empathy over ego. There's no "I'll focus on myself when we end police brutality. That's just more important right now". The inner and outer work is all the work. It's a package deal because one cannot be successful without the other. Our work will be that of constantly toggling between requiring others to come up higher and also challenging ourselves to do the same. This is the flow of exchange in the life of growth minded people and if anyone should be of a growth mindset, it should be those of us who say we want to Be The Change.

This work, though necessary, is not for the faint of heart. It's not for the humblebrags or the glory hogs that want to receive an award for every good deed they do. And it's not for those who keep doing the work, as long as it continues to make them feel good. Anyone who's made the intellectual decision to choose diversity, over division, can attest to how the work is both meaningful and messy. Just because your mind chooses a thing, doesn't mean all of the other areas of you just get in line with your decision. It's like when a child first becomes aware that Santa Clause isn't real and then begins to connect the dots of what's really happening behind the scenes at Christmas time. It's not unusual for children to experience a flood of emotions when realizing that everything they thought they knew about Christmas is not real and in that moment of realization, that child loses some of their childlike innocence. The revelation of the reality of racism and privilege can have the same effect on adults. Head knowledge doesn't automatically override the stories we've adopted as truth our whole lives. This is part of what creates the tension so many feel, when racism goes from concept to reality and hits close to home. If anything, our initial response is to fight to save our innocence and to preserve the familiar that has shaped the way we have seen the world.

The growing sentiment that I'm hearing right now from people who are doing the work of creating change, challenging their own comfort zones, and fighting for justice, is that they just can't help but feel angry all the time. In fact, at times, it seems as if they are consumed by it. Though it is exhausting and they would like a break from this new found constant boil of anger, in the back of their minds they're wondering "But if I'm not angry about what's happening in the world, then who will be?" It's an age-old question those who have been angry about racism have been asking themselves for generations: "Why aren't more people outraged by this?" There are those who have been angry for so long that the concept of feeling any peace might as well be explained in the same terms you would talk about the existence of unicorns. It's a nice thing to dream about, but we don't live in dreams, we live in the world we're experiencing right now. In many ways it can feel as if allowing yourself to feel anything other than anger is a betrayal to the Black community or to anti-racist efforts.

I can speak for myself when I say that my own anger has been at an all-time high these past few months, and I'm brought to tears much quicker than I used to be. I feel as if my emotional fuse is so short. When I was younger, I had a short temper, much of it was a symptom of some unprocessed losses I had experienced in my life. As an adult I'm usually pretty even keeled emotionally and it takes very specific things to create emotional waves. Of course, since COVID-19 began making a real impact on life, then the racial upheaval sparked by George Floyd's death, my emotional baseline has felt like it's in a constant state of irritation that fluctuates between anger and sadness at any given point throughout the day. My ego almost gets in the way of admitting this because I enjoy being more emotionally balanced! It's more in alignment with what feels right for me, but this is actually a great example of privilege in action. When I choose to close my eyes to the hurt and harm of others because it disturbs the comfort bubble that I've been living in, then I am letting my privilege of even having a comfort bubble that I can go to, keep me from creating community. Closing our eyes to another person's pain because it will disturb our peace doesn't necessarily mean we hate those people we're turning a blind eye to.

I mean, we don't give money to every homeless person asking for change on the street and we certainly don't donate to every cause that exists - unless we want to go broke. So, it makes sense that we can still be good people, while not having the bandwidth for every hurting person in the world. What I'm referring to isn't the inability to shoulder the pain of the entire world, because literally no one can do that. What I'm referring to, is when you choose to live your life in a way that prioritizes your experiences over others. When it's easier to deny other people's experiences because of how uncomfortable the awareness of their life makes you feel because it requires you to take a look at your own. You may have the physical ability to say with your lips "I love all people" but if you live your life unwilling to hold space for anyone else's truth but your own, then your kind of love is both conditional and not living to its fullest potential.

You love all people in theory, but not really in action. A love that can only can be heard but not seen or felt is as useful as a cure for cancer that's been created but won't be accessible for another decade. It sure sounds nice, but has no real value to anyone who is suffering right now. While you love in theory, people are being murdered in practice. While you love only with words, people are being shot with bullets. While you enjoy a chat about how scary the world is with your friends over a glass of wine, immigrant children are being held in cages, separated from their parents. All of this is happening every day and yet there are those who are offended by anyone who calls attention to the fact that there's such a thing as privilege. There are those so attached to the rightness they've experienced as part of their privilege that instead of seeking understanding and exploring their disconnect, they would rather silence the voice that threatens their comfort. This is the America we all share and yet only a select group experiences and feels the effects of its social injustices, because not everyone has the luxury of living without being touched by them.

A prime example of privilege prioritizing itself over understanding, is when the comeback to any message related to how Black lives matter is "White lives matter!" We read it in the comment section of social media posts, we hear it in hostile conversations, and we've seen it on the news. This proclamation and is very seldom posed as a genuine concern of feeling as if their value as a white person is being diminished. If someone were to respond to "Black lives matter" with "They do, but sometimes I feel confused as to what the real meaning is behind this message. I know you want your life to matter, but so does my life and so does the life of my family. Do you feel that because I'm white and because of the privilege that white people have had, that my life should lower in value to make you feel more valuable? Because that doesn't feel right to me either". That would be so much more empowering a statement because of the opportunity for dialogue that it creates rather than using "white lives matter" with the same connotation as an insult. Regardless of if you would consider this to be an ideal response or not, responding in any way remotely close to this holds space for way more understanding and community than just saying "White lives matter" to anything that calls white privilege into accountability.

I'm well aware that this kind of response will feel farfetched for some of you because this kind of response, unfortunately, tends to be the exception, not the rule. Although I know it may not be typical, it is not inconceivable. Is this a perfect anti-racist response? No. It is however a vulnerable one and I believe that vulnerability is the special sauce that's missing in a lot of the more hostile, or defensive, exchanges that you see between communities that are different from one another. Vulnerability requires honesty and it's difficult to be vulnerable when you're unwilling to acknowledge your own flaws or admit you don't know it all. Though vulnerability exposes you, so does hate. You expose what you're made of when you are vulnerable and you expose what you're made of when you spew hate. Both require you to muster up energy, but only one has the potential to pour energy back into you equal to, or greater than, what it initially required. It's up to you to decide how you choose to expose yourself and which kind of energy you want to produce in order to do it.

I believe that so much of the hostility comes as a result of the white community hearing "Black lives matter" and they either take it as a direct representation of the Black Lives Matter organization or they translate "Black lives matter" into "White lives don't matter". They have the argument that the BLM movement is totally political and has nothing to do with us actually caring about our community, When I say "Black lives matter" it is neither tied to the organization, nor a statement to minimize the white experience. When I say "Black lives matter" my intent is that it is a call to action. It is like the order to march given to a soldier. The organization has played its part in creating the statement, but it's been all of us that's brought the statement to life and have given it the ability to move across the world. This is what I've tried to explain to those who choose to believe that BLM is solely a political agenda and is not, in fact, powered by people's desire to be treated justly.

During a moment when a Michigan business owner was getting backlash for accidentally sharing some borderline racist views on their business Facebook page, someone I knew shared a graphic in response to the news story that said BLM was a lie because "If Black lives really mattered then they'd stop shooting each other". As much of a deflective response as that was, at no point should the violence of any community be a reason to ever imply that they don't deserve to advocate for the validity of their existence. If there are those who want to use this as a believable argument, then it's also believable that "White lives matter" is also a lie. There are white people killing other white people. So, does every case of white-on-white violence mean that the white community doesn't actually care about themselves? And is any attempt at advocating for their community to be safe and healthy a moot point? What about the findings of the 2018 Child Maltreatment report put out by the Children's Bureau that shows that 49.6% of child maltreatment perpetrators are white? [1](U.S Department of Health and Human Services 2018) Would Black people be right to say "How can they say white lives matter, when they are literally beating their white future"? I'm going to go out on a limb and bet that a statement like that would not sit well or be well received if it was the only retort given to white people when their main objective is to fight for justice and not be afraid for their life.

I believe that Black lives matter and I also advocate for all lives. Anytime someone wants to yell "white lives matter!!" as a comeback to any talk about Black lives, my natural response is "They absolutely do". The difference is that this country wasn't created at the expense of your life. We didn't hang you from trees. We didn't steal you from your home and bring you to ours to serve us, to be raped by us, and to be sold by us. You haven't had to live in the United States with the reality that only about 70 years ago were we given legal freedom to eat where we wanted. Having legal permission is not the same as being allowed to by individuals and communities. Those are just facts. Forget feelings. Those are the facts. If the tables were turned, if my Black privilege was instrumental in keeping you from feeling safe and truly a part of this country you helped create, and you finally found your voice to make sure people knew something had to change, I would probably feel a sense of discomfort as well. I think we all have a responsibility to each other. To make sure as a whole we are healthy, protected, loved, and thriving. That's personally what I'm fighting for and what I'm inviting all of you to lean into as well. Part of what makes racism so dangerous is that it is the complete opposite of humanitarianism in that it doesn't see life and existence, it only sees difference. Racism in all its various forms desensitizes the one practicing it every time we make our sense of identity the center of someone else's need to be valued. It's not about us and if we bring it back to us every time someone says "please see me" then there will always be too tall a wall between us to ever see life from their perspective. We can all love and value who we are and yet also engage in conversation about how we may be playing a role in either, adding to or taking away from, the value of another. Why do so many of us feel we have to go to such extremes of either denying ourselves and accepting another or denying another and accepting ourselves? This is not an either/or situation! You can absolutely have your cake and eat it too when it comes to celebrating and acknowledging the life, history, and culture of ourselves and those around us. So much of our worldview may have been founded on the idea of racial hierarchy and that certain lives have more value than others. That doesn't have to be the world we continue to create. Hierarchy is such a convenient system to put in place when you are the dominant community, but today, today we all have platforms that we can use to give life to our voice. Things are still so incredibly imbalanced, but the same social platforms that give hate a broader reach, also has the power to amplify the voices of those passionate about equality - if we choose to be intentional about not just being "not racist" but anti-racist.

In every respect you should feel uncomfortable about anything that is in opposition of the life, health, and protection of marginalized people. You should be angry about people hanging other people from trees because they are Black, and people spitting on other people because they are immigrants or perceived to be. You should feel unsettled that some of the very law enforcement that is supposed to protect all men are infiltrated with some who perpetuate unlawful violence against people because of their skin color. You shouldn't feel peace if the leadership of this country publicly (or privately) expresses racist ideas toward the people that live in it. These things should upset you; I know they sure do upset me!

It stresses me out when my social media feeds are flooded with story after story of Black deaths as a result of racism, immigrants and their families being housed like dogs, women being raped, and their outfit choice being blamed for the reason it happened. I'm angered by the police brutality against protesters - protesting against police brutality. I'm noticing how tightly I'm clenching my jaw even now! It's hard not to feel a storm raging inside you when there's so much inequality and injustice around every corner and you feel overwhelmed trying to figure out what your role is to be in all of it. So many of us are so angry and some of you are just beginning to realize there's something to be angry about. I think that where a lot of the exhaustion and inner turmoil comes from during times of prolonged anger is when we begin to believe that anger is the only confirmation of disagreement, when in reality it is not. Anger has a deceptive way of making us believe it is the most productive emotion. This is not always the case even though it's sometimes the easier default emotion. You recognize this truth if you've ever had your heart broken by someone. It feels better to be angry at them than to be hurt. It feels better to scream and throw things than to sit with the disappointment of another failed relationship. With injustice it's easier to feel angry than to feel afraid and it's easier to feel enraged than to process feelings of uncertainty of what the future looks like. Anger plays a necessary role in change but so does joy, peace, gratitude, hope, and love, as well as a slew of other inner sources for inspiration to work toward change. You can have peace and do anti-racist work. You can be both grateful and passionate about changing policies. You can confront biases from a place of love and still spark change. As much as it feels like anger is an outlet that you can source all of this energy from, though it can be momentarily, it is not sustainable without a cost. Prolonged anger will give you the passionate energy you need to get started and even get some progress, but it'll eventually short circuit the parts of you needed to stay in tune with the heart of the mission: People.

Soon enough, if you don't diversify the sources of your energy, your anger will become your mission. Soon your anger will become the work. Desensitization doesn't just apply to when people become desensitized to violence or death. People can become desensitized to hope and peace as well if they allow their heart to be steeped in anger for too long. Anger is not the only thing that differentiates a committed advocate from a pacified one, and anger is not the most important part of the work. At the end of the day, the fight for social justice may start out in anger, but it has to take a more holistic approach long term. One that incorporates more than just running on emotion in order for the work to be sustained.

This work is an inside job. It starts with challenging how we see the world and why we see the world the way we do. It starts with asking ourselves why we feel so uncomfortable when a Black person walks into the store we work at or why we're apprehensive to greet the white stranger that walks through the doors of our all-Black church on a Sunday morning. It starts inside our homes by teaching our children to acknowledge differences, but not be afraid of them, empowering them to be lifelong learners from people different from them, and making sure that we as adults are living examples of that to them. It starts with challenging what we believe and why we believe it. How did we learn what we live? Was it taught to us? If it was taught, have we questioned if we truly resonate with these beliefs anymore or if we primarily project the beliefs of others without exploring what we want our experience in the world to look like? I've said it before and I'll say it again, this is deep work we have to do if we really want something different than what we've experienced in the past and are experiencing now.

It's okay if you feel the weight of the inner dialogue I'm inviting you to engage in, because I do too. It's okay if it makes you feel uncomfortable just thinking about what asking yourself these questions could unearth because I share in your discomfort. This stuff is the hard stuff because when initiating self-reflection and challenging what you've been going with the flow of, you may end up shedding light on so much more than you initially set out to discover. When we get curious about ourselves and look at our inner life with childlike curiosity and ask "But why?" you may end up disrupting the very foundational beliefs you've built your sense of community and normalcy on. Much like when a parent is challenged with a question from their child that they would rather avoid, they deflect because they don't want to admit that they really don't know what to say in response. Our egos, and even the people close to us, may start to have a similar reaction to our search for truth: To avoid, deflect, and deny.

This is the moment when you are confronted with asking yourself if your commitment lies solely with your community or with creating community as a whole.

There's no rule of humanity that says in order to successfully create a safe community for all you have to abandon the community you've always known. People may try to make you feel that way, systems may try to paint a picture that this is the way it needs to be, but you can absolutely have a local community that you love while trying to build a global one that you can be proud of. The two are not mutually exclusive, although social injustice and racism are able to exist because people have used race and ethnicity as a way to compartmentalize communities, innately pinning them against one another. This has been the way, but it doesn't have to continue to be the way.

I hear this inner conflict between loyalty to the community you know and passion for the community we need so often these days. Those who are white wanting to stand with the Black community, while also feeling conflicted because so much of the turmoil they are speaking out against has to do with the hate that people who look like them are perpetuating. There's a tug of war going on inside many where they are wondering who or what is the actual enemy. Is it racism? White privilege? Politics? Law enforcement? It can also be hard for some to draw a distinction between whiteness and racism when so much of the hate that's being recorded is from white people to Black people. I would imagine that some of the white community that chooses not to take a solid stand either way, do so because they are conflicted with how they go about taking a stand for equality and taking what feels like a stand against their entire community. This has the potential to be an incredibly jarring experience if you do not have a strong sense of self or support from like-minded individuals. Even for those who do have a more fully formed sense of who they are as individuals it can be unnerving. Because of this I empathize with those walking laps in this race instead of running. You have to start somewhere and at some level of imperfection. Just know that at some point you have to graduate to the next level of commitment to equality because those who don't ever fully commit to their role run the risk of eventually bowing out due to not having enough energy invested in purpose.

I believe this question of where our loyalties lie plays a part in the inner life of some Black people too. There are those of us who have white friends that we adore and that have been nothing but good to us. We've had no reason to feel any disdain for their whiteness. Some of these same people are like family to us and then there are others who are actually our family. What does advocating for our lives as Black people and fighting against systemic racism look like, when the systems so often look like the very people we know and love? What about those of us that have friends or family that are in law enforcement? What does holding space for both even look like? I know I struggle with this myself sometimes when I'm talking to friends that are trying to understand how I must be feeling.

I want to say "I'm so tired of living in primarily white communities where people either fawn all over me like an exotic animal in the wild, or they avoid me. I want to feel like a normal person and not made to feel like I deserve some kind of award for being a Black professional, as if I'm some kind of anomaly. I'm tired of people making a case that Black people need to live in the present because slavery was so long ago. I'm angry that so many in my community get knots in their stomachs when a law enforcement vehicle is behind them, not because they knew they were speeding, but because they know that too often law enforcement has proven to not need a reason to pull over people of color".

Those are the things I want to say. Yet in the moment, as I look into my friend's eyes, while they wait for me to share my heart with them, 9 times out of 10, I hold back and give them 30% of my truth. I know they love me; I know they hurt for me, and I know they feel helpless. Yet, as much as I would like to give them a play by play on what my community is going through and how it's tearing me up inside, there always feels like there is this invisible line that as a Black person I'm usually walking on but rarely crossing. It's the line between speaking truth and burning bridges. I would love to say that there's a distinct difference between the two, but when it comes to the topic of racism, the line can easily get very blurry. The topic of racism stings and although the Black community has felt this sting for generations and the topic has never left our lips, for those who are the majority, there are many of them that haven't had to have racism be a theme in their life. Yes, of course it's always existed and to those who are aware of its vicious realities it seems outlandish that there are people who just don't get it. This is the definition of privilege. Our inability to escape certain realities doesn't change the fact that there are many who had the luxury of hiding from them. So, when I consider this, sometimes sharing the other 70% of my truth feels too heavy to me. It feels too much of a burden, not only to share, but to try and enlighten someone about, especially if you know that their primary Black experience is you. I feel that if my truth is too heavy for me, and I've been living with it my whole life, then will they be crushed under the weight of it? Not having awareness of the truth makes them privileged and me treating them like they're too delicate to handle the truth, keeps them privileged. This is the cycle myself and other people of color sometimes struggle with. I am strong because I've had to be, but I have not always felt sure. Am I alone in this?

I share these truths about myself not without reservation, but with enough resolve to make any scrutiny I may receive worth it. This vulnerability is part of my inside job. This book is part of my work. The tough love, the harsh truths, and the hard realities throughout this chapter are invitations to lean into your inside work, whatever it may be, because we all have some to be done. I invite you to do it honestly, do it authentically, and do it knowing that you may not feel brave right now, but every action builds on the other until one day your courage outranks your fear. As Brené Brown said in her book *Daring Greatly: How the Courage to Be Vulnerable Transforms the Way We Live, Love, Parent, and Lead,* "When we spend our lives waiting until we're perfect or bulletproof before we walk into the arena, we ultimately sacrifice relationships and opportunities that may not be recoverable, we squander our precious time, and we turn our backs on our gifts, those unique contributions that only we can make. Perfect and bulletproof are seductive, but they don't exist in the human experience."

NINE - Time is Up

As we continue to delve deeper into the great disparity between the white and Black experience of justice in America, I've noticed there is a shared thought amongst some that has been projected onto Black people a lot lately. In response to all of the advocacy efforts going on, some say that since slavery happened so long ago, Black people need to get over it. It seems to me the consensus is that by drawing attention to the historic account and current continuance of oppression, that we are playing victim to what we now have control over. It's said by some that drawing attention to the past is a way for the Black community to not take responsibility for their own lives and to place the fault of their position on the white community. Some even say that biases are something we should just choose to rise above and if we don't, it's because we don't want to. The sentiment "We all have struggles that we have to overcome. I've overcome mine and Black people just need to overcome theirs" is thrown around sometimes with a sense of indignation and at other times under the guise of concern. Like when someone asks you how you're doing, but they don't actually care.

I wonder if we'd tell a woman we know and love, "It happened so long ago, it's time to get over it" when she is crying on our shoulder because she's still mourning the loss of a pregnancy from years ago - even though she has had successful pregnancies since then. What if someone in your family had experienced a sexual assault and you were expressing to a friend how heartbroken you were over it? Would you accept, "Why are you so upset about it? It happened to someone else, not you" as a plausible argument for why you shouldn't be bothered by it?

Trauma is not an isolated thing and it isn't always brought on by extreme experiences. Sometimes traumas creep up inside you while you're just living your life and thinking something you've experienced is "normal". And it's not until years go by that you became aware of how that exchange affected how you interact with the world. Trauma's effects do not just end at the person who is experiencing them firsthand. If that was the case, there would be no such situations as generations of child abuse running through families where the Grandfather abused his son, the son abused his daughter, and the daughter abused her children. The abuse instead would have started and stopped at the Grandfather. If trauma was isolated, then there would be no such thing as PTSD. If trauma was an isolated thing then the concept of "emotional baggage" would be something that wouldn't be all that commonly understood because we wouldn't still be carrying things that happened to us long ago, we would have just let it happen and then let it go. It's a nice thought though, the idea of trauma being isolated and of us never having to relive anything. It's nice to think of a world in which we are all emotionally and psychologically whole and healthy, and where so many of us aren't living with the evidence of the traumas of those around us, as well as traumas that have affected us directly. Unfortunately, trauma has always been a part of the human experience because we are not made of steel and our hearts are not protected by brick walls, no matter how tough we like to believe we are.

It is said that you can define trauma as an emotional upset. Well, if that's not the most underwhelming definition you ever did read, then I don't know what is! All you need in order to have had experienced trauma, is to have experienced an emotional upset. This definition does not go on to explain that a trauma can only be caused by very significant upsets like that caused by abuse or witnessing a murder. It does not go on to say that the emotional upset can only be defined as a trauma if it was something that only you directly experienced. It does not even define the timeline in which the emotional upset has to occur in order for it to be truly considered a trauma. It just defines it as "an emotional upset". How is it that a definition, words on a page, seem to give more space to validate people's traumas than some people give for people's traumas?

People all across the country have been emotionally upset during COVID-19, when states had been on lockdown and the closing of hair salons had people hitting the streets with protest signs that read "I want a haircut!" People all across the country have been emotionally upset because they're being required to wear a mask to keep themselves and other people safe in public spaces, and many have expressed their upset by verbally or physically assaulting grocery store employees whose jobs were only to enforce the rules. Parents all across the country are emotionally upset because going to school looks so different now for their children and they are torn between sending them to school and exposing them to the virus, or trying to decide how they are going to manage homeschool while working to provide for their family. If trauma is defined by being emotionally upset, then in some way, whether big or small, COVID-19 has caused us all some trauma. Yet, no matter what extremes people go through in order to exercise their "rights", no matter how they express themselves or how nasty they get in the comment section, there is still some level of validation and empathy that's given to them by way of "I understand why they're upset though. I don't like it either". It's the power of the shared experience. In some cases, it's even a great example of the phrase "misery loves company". It's a little easier for us to make some allowances for people that are expressing trauma from COVID-19 because we are all experiencing the effects of it. When someone expresses upset, or they act out because they are sick of wearing masks, or they lash out online at a Governor for adding more restrictions, you may express that you think their reaction is too extreme but it's usually followed with some kind of sentiment that sounds like "But I understand because….". It's much easier for us to make certain allowances for a plethora of people's behaviors when we have a shared experience with them.

With racism and discrimination, the reality is that it simply isn't a shared experience for everyone. It's harder for many people to find something they can understand about it. It's harder to make allowances for behaviors that result from it if you've never experienced it. It's harder to identify the intention of someone, if you don't know what it's like to live a life in which these are realities and are things that shape the way you see the world. Why is it that someone can call their Governor a tyrant for placing restrictions to help keep Americans safe and people more readily support that, but when someone calls a law enforcement officer a racist as a result of their blatant display of racism, they are considered anti-American? Is it not considered anti-American to refuse and constantly fight what's necessary to keep America safe? When someone throws an attitude with a gas station attendant because they're told they need to wear a mask due to a state mandate, whether you agree with them or not, there is still a level of empathy for them because wearing masks is inconvenient for us all. However, when people speak up about the just or unjust treatment of people of color, they're berated with hate and annoyance no matter the way they deliver their thoughts. When did our priorities get so out of whack? When did our internal compass begin to point toward prioritizing the "need" for haircuts and away from the need for human rights?

Black people are often labeled as having a victim mentality and yet we tolerate the exaggerated complaints of entitled people who don't want anyone telling them to wear a dang mask if it doesn't serve them. If we ever dared to go into the lion's den and accuse such people of having a victim mentality, we would be verbally crucified, because to them their suffering is real. Their suffering is real to them because they feel it, whether we believe it is merited or not. Well, our suffering is real too and yet the Black community is told "the only people placing limits on you is yourself" and "get over it, slavery is a thing of the past". So, my question to you would be, "Is it really though?" Is slavery truly and completely a thing of the past? It's true that we no longer have shackles placed on our hands and feet, but when the advocacy efforts increased so did the reports of Black men found hanging from trees. Yet, people want to say that we have no reason to feel on guard. I ask you, are the symptoms of slavery truly no longer present today? We may not have men or women that we call "Master "anymore, but still today in the United States there are people that chastise Black adult men and call them "Boy". This was a term used to call Black men in the days of slavery and continued on as part of the racial etiquette during the time of Jim Crow laws. Is the stain of slavery really washed from this nation? In June of 2020 a conversation between some white law enforcement officers in North Carolina was brought to light that stated they wanted to "start slaughtering them f------ n------". [2](Elfrink, Morning Mix 2020) Is slavery really a thing of the past? From where I'm standing all of these things are reminiscent of how slaves and other Black people have been treated before and after emancipation. Stick a price tag on us all today and you've got a modern day slave trade. Slavery by its fullest definition is legally abolished, but the need that many have to still rule over Black people has not in its totality left this country. As long as racism cannot let go of wanting us enslaved, or worse dead, then we as a people will refuse to forget that we did not and do not deserve such treatment.

If I sound upset, it's because I am. If I sound exasperated, it's because I am. I am more conscious than ever that my brown skin is seen as offensive to some people. I am more aware than ever that I don't want to go to the grocery store alone as it's getting darker in the small primarily white town that I currently live in. I feel much less at ease about going off the beaten path at the beach or driving through small Michigan towns that I'm not familiar with. I feel less unsure about dating white men than I used to. I look over my shoulder more. I take more notice of activity around me that seems unusual. My stomach turns when I notice a police officer behind me, even though I've done nothing wrong. Whereas before, my knee jerk reaction would be to take a quick glance at my speedometer. Some of the peace that I had previously known has been disrupted because there are white people that want to retaliate using any Black life that might be an easy target. There are people in law enforcement that want to flex their authority on people of color because they feel backed into a corner since law enforcement practices have been under a public microscope. There are white people that do not like having their privilege challenged, do not like feeling as if the Black community is getting so much attention, and they want to keep the scales imbalanced and in their favor. Not everyone wants equality. Those who want to keep a world that is run by a racial hierarchy are teachers, pastors, brothers, friends, lawyers, Moms and Dads, politicians, and janitors. They are just people that we interact with every day. As a Black person in a world where you are the minority, we have reason to be hyperaware. The thing that baffles me is, there are some who reason that white people wouldn't feel hostile toward Black people if we just didn't start this "Black

Lives Matter thing". The argument from some is that if we would have just kept our mouths shut and stayed in our lane, there wouldn't be a problem. If we just left well enough alone and didn't stir the pot then there wouldn't be an issue. If we would just be happy with what we've got and didn't get greedy then people wouldn't be mad at us. These are actual comments that I heard with my own ears from hushed conversations between like minds.

This is why we're upset. This is why we protest. This is why we say with raised voices and raised fists that "Black lives matter!" It's not because we don't believe that white lives matter. It's not because we believe that all police officers everywhere are corrupt. It's not because we are playing victim to the past. It's not because we are greedy and are not thankful for what progress in equality has been made thus far. We're upset because we are tired of having to fight tooth and nail for what systems have created as given rights that most white Americans have always just been entitled to, but that help to perpetuate division and a hierarchical society. We're upset because what has been considered rights for many, have often seemed to be gifts of charity for all the rest of us who are not straight white tow-the-line people. By most American standards, rights are something you're entitled to. For the rest of us our rights are something we should be grateful for when we get them. Rights for many, are something that should be demanded. Yet, the petition for the rights of those not a part of the majority, should be a polite request. If our request is turned down then we should not shout, we should not demand, we should not protest, we should not cry, we should not fight, we should not question why, we should not advocate for ourselves, because to do so is to be an enemy of normalcy. To do so is to be an enemy of how it's always been. Well my friend, time is up.

Time is up on creating a hierarchy out of our differences. Time is up on blaming the people being assaulted by racism and limited by discriminating policies, when we should be educating people on how to be anti-racist and spark change. Time. Is. Up. We are so much more than the physical, psychological, and emotional upsets we've experienced or are experiencing right now. We are so much more than our trauma. We are more than the definitions others may use to define us and we are even more than the definitions we've created for ourselves. We are resilient and we are still here. The stories of our history, our present, and our hope of a great legacy are ours to tell, experience, and create. We are not victims because labeling ourselves as victims implies that we have lost, which we have not. We are not victims of oppression; we are victors of equality...and equality is **our right.**

TEN - In a Sea of Voices

For those Black persons who may have read this book and felt disconnected from its message, I thank you. I thank you for not tuning me out, even if you don't agree or share my viewpoint. I value the time you committed to finishing this book and not just writing it off at the moment you felt like I wasn't speaking to you. I am not so naive to believe that I could speak for the entire Black community, though there was a time when I did think this was the case. Life, coupled with my journey of having to unlearn some things, has taught me otherwise. I am not the voice for us all because there are too many shoes I have not walked in, too many experiences I have not had, and too many people I have not yet met. Even when we cannot see eye to eye with another Black person or even when we feel like someone is being too harsh or too lenient, we really need to try to be present and keep listening. We must keep engagement. We must keep showing up. No one person can be the entire voice of the Black community, trying to require that of someone else or ourselves is discounting all of the stories from millions of Black people that we have never met. I am but one voice in a sea of voices, but together, if all of us shared our stories and if all of us used the platforms that we have, collectively we can create The Black Story. One that is as diverse as the shades of our skin, colors of our eyes, and textures of our hair. You may not think so but you need my story and I need yours. We are each other's teachers as our ancestors have been ours and we will be the future's.

The topic of racism is so grand, so diverse, and so layered that there is bound to be both an alignment and mismatching of opinions on all sides. No matter what walk of life you come from, we all have some measure of the weight of what we've been through and the dream of what we hope for battling it out within us. This inner conflict is bound to happen in a world where we see both great brutality and great humanity being played out in front of our very eyes on a daily basis.

I'm writing this book during a social, political, and racial uprising. We're coming up on one of the most pivotal presidential elections in my lifetime, where we are faced with the choice to draw from a tumultuous racial past in order to Make America Great for Some or to draw inspiration from our future in order to Make America Great for All. The #BlackLivesMatter movement is at the climax of its influence currently. At the time that I'm writing this, on Wednesday June 3rd, 2020, I am witnessing the most large-scale show of support for the Black community that I have ever seen before. Across different communities, races, generations, and socioeconomic groups the support is loud, proud, and tangible. It's truly amazing, overwhelming, and is bringing me to tears just talking about it. Even with the overwhelming support, the Black community is still under attack. There have been Snapchats and social media posts with the hashtag #GeorgeFloydChallenge in which young white people mock the murder of George Floyd by posing on the ground with their knee on a friend's neck. We have people unashamedly claiming their desire for all Black people to be wiped off the planet, and we're still being shot at unnecessarily by law enforcement in contrast to others who have been shown much more leniency. Our community is riddled with allies and enemies, just like it always has been, but I choose to believe that right now those with us outnumber those against us. Or at least those with us are making the loudest noise.

As we experience these extraordinary times, as we witness the outpour of love and support for the Black community, and as we see the wheels of change start to turn, I can't help but ask myself: How long will this fire burn? If history repeats itself, the fire and passion that the entire nation is running on right now will begin to short circuit. We have already seen some of that begin to happen. I too have felt myself becoming exhausted and spent. Part of it is just a matter of what realistically the human psyche and body can handle. Can we sustain this momentum while also preserving the energy we need to see things through? I'm optimistic. I believe that if we have enough people who stay in the game, we can keep the momentum going. When some need to take a break and recharge, then others will step in and continue the work, and ideally that would be the exchange of energy until we make more and more progress. My hope is that we will be able to keep enough people engaged in the mission in order to keep putting in the work, long term.

To have any hope of turning this moment into a movement

that we can build upon for years to come, it's going to take more than just us being the loudest voice in the room or the ones that make the most noise. Being loud is not synonymous with being heard. If you've ever been in an argument with someone who tried to get their point across by getting louder and raising their voice over yours, you know that being the loudest in the room does not mean that you are being heard! Personally, when people start to do that to me I either go quiet because at this point, I just want whatever this exchange, is to be done or I get defensive and loud right back at them. At that point, the meaning behind the words is lost and everything left is just a disturbance. At this moment many of us are disturbing the peace with our cries for accountability by banging our fists on the doors of injustice and stomping our feet as we march down the streets of our communities. This is the time for disturbance, to be seen, and for us to be reminded that if racism is loud, then we will be louder. We also need to be purposeful in expanding our advocacy practices to include intimate dialogue with those of sameness, as well as with those different from us. Getting involved with community committees or organizations, advocating for policy changes at our jobs, speaking up at the moment discrimination or racism is at play, and continually learning and educating ourselves is how it gets done. Protesting is beautiful and meaningful in so many ways, but personally I feel that the real risk comes in times of close conversation and vulnerable engagement. When you use words fueled, not only by your emotion and passion but by intentionality, that's when what you're doing or saying creates opportunities for all involved to expose blindspots. This, I believe, is where the magic happens in all relationships and within many types of division. When I was in my early 20s and going through a divorce, I started seeing a therapist who made a statement about disputes within marriage that I have never forgotten. It was that, when it came to disagreements within my marriage they were always made up of his side, her side, and the truth. No matter if it's a romantic relationship, a family dispute, a coworker disagreement, or a heated discussion about racism, there are always multiple sides, multiple stories and experiences, and then there is the truth. Sometimes it's harder than others to distinguish what the truth is apart from the stories and point of views that are shared, but it's important to always consider that all three are present and should be acknowledged. This is one of the foundational cornerstones of building a diverse community of people who bring their own experiences to the world but also want to move it in the same direction. While we work to marry what we want, with what we're actually accomplishing, we must in some ways begin to flesh out when to prioritize collaboration over rightness for the sake of forward movement. I'm not proposing that we make any concessions for racism, murder, or injustice. I'm saying that as we pursue coming together to right these wrongs, we will have to confront ourselves and each other's stories in order to stay together. In order to achieve staying together we will have to challenge our commitment to our own rightness in the pursuit of being collaborators of unity and justice.

By the time this book is published and in front of the eyes of those willing to read it, I wonder where the energy will be by then? I wonder, if this book will be so fortunate to have its words live on long past my lifetime. How much progress in racial justice and equality will there be? I wonder if 100 years from now people will read this book and think "Wow, it's so interesting getting a glimpse into her life and reading some of the experiences she had while living through the COVID-19 pandemic and 2020. What a time it must have been to be alive during that!" Or will they wonder "Man! Here we are 100 years later and we're still divided. We're still fighting for the equal rights of Black and brown people! What a shame." Of course, I hope and I pray that everything myself and so many others are advocating for will not be for nothing. I hope the future will look back at the past and say "Because of you we are not only free but we are thriving". That is the hope I choose to live with in the midst of a whole lot of uncertainty. It's so easy to disassociate when we speak in terms of the future and the past, but in this particular instance when I refer to the past, I am speaking of us. You and I are the future's past being played out in the present.

What we do or don't do, what we say or don't say, the ways we make every day count or the ways we waste the days solely on ourselves, will be the past that the future will reap the benefits - or consequences of. We have lived for ourselves alone for long enough. Our society is living proof of that. There was a point in time where there was more of a sense of people feeling responsible for the health and wellness of not just those closest to them, but to strangers too. Somewhere along the way we lost that sense of responsibility for one another. I have a feeling we lost it somewhere between the time we started to become entertained by murder counts on the news, like you would keep score of the touchdowns in a football game. I feel we have lost our way from one another in so many ways, but I believe that if we draw inspiration from the future outcome of our current actions then we can begin to rebuild the sense of community that has been torn down brick by brick over the years.

I lived wrapped up in myself for far too long too. I thought I loved people and I thought I was a humanitarian, but honestly, I was the laziest version of both. I did just enough to feel good about myself and to look great to those around me, many of whom had placed a ceiling on their efforts as well. I wasn't always like that though, that's the puzzling thing to me. There was a time years ago, when I strongly advocated for those who were being treated unfairly. I spoke up against imbalance in my church, at my school, at home, at work, and often I didn't think twice about advocating for my own fair treatment. I quickly found out that for me, bravery and being a Black female often meant you had a target on your back, and the unfortunate reality was that often those aiming at it would be the ones you thought would have your back - not stab you in it.

I was encouraged in church to use my God-given giftings and was applauded when they painted pretty pictures and created warm fuzzies, but when I allowed God to lead my voice and I strayed from inspiration to edification, then it became clear that I needed to be silenced. The boldness, bravery, and discernment that was developing within me proved to be a threat to ego and in many ways, I was being bullied into choosing conformity over individuality. I was being punished for not using what was God-given for man's own intentions. Though I chose to leave that specific church instead of conforming and then found a community that supported my individuality more, the imprint of that long season of my life stayed with me, even up until recently. I honestly didn't even realize how many areas of myself and how many of my hopes I had shut down because of the bullying that I endured in the church I grew up in. I had, little by little, allowed parts of myself to fade into the background. This is one of those sneaky effects of trauma that I was talking about. I eventually forgot what thriving as a unique individual looked like. How sad is that? No one, and I mean no one, should be made to believe that who they are should be snuffed out, not because they are causing harm to anyone but because their personhood is a threat to traditionalism. Isn't that what fear and hatred is to so many? A tradition that has been passed down through generations? Like the passing down of a pearl necklace to every daughter on their wedding day or having all the men in the family attend opening day every year. Fear is handed down to people as they attend hate-rallies disguised as family dinners and Sunday service.

These traditions unfortunately have been, and are still being practiced in communities across the globe. Whether white, Black, Latinx, Asian, or of other descent, people have imposed their fear and hatred for bodies different from their own, onto other people for generations. Some at greater detriments than others as can be seen by the history of slaughtered Native Americans, the Holocaust, and the slavery of African people. These are just a few examples of genocides and the suppression of people groups that have occurred in the world. Even when what you're perpetuating, or what you're experiencing, isn't any of these extremes the starting point is always the same.

White people often fear Black people because that's what they've been taught to do. If you weren't brought up in a community where you were taught fear, then you are one of the fortunate ones. Even for those who are white and had parents who taught them to love everyone the same and to "not see skin color", the general population of sameness often still spoke of the perceived danger of Black people to them. Sometimes, spoken in the same terms you would use in order to convince someone that ghosts exist. I've heard the stories told to me so many times. The plight of the person who grew up gravitating toward those who were different from them, to be met with some level of awestruck wonder from those of sameness, as if they had just witnessed someone befriending a tiger in the wild. I've had white people tell me stories of how their friends would say things like "I didn't know you liked Black people". They would lose friends because they didn't just go along with the discriminatory comments that would be made in certain social circles they were a part of. It's the fear of ending the tradition of fear, that is often just too hard for people to accept. Even suggesting that they consider separating from their tradition of fear can feel as if you were asking them to pluck out the very eyes they use to see the world every day.

Like those who have been taught to fear, many Black people have lived in suspicion of white people because we have been taught to. Many still feel the sting of the whip on our ancestors backs and yet the wounds cannot be seen on our skin for they are felt in our hearts. If we don't assimilate then, it's as if we have no choice but to internalize the fear that is reflected back at us by the facial expressions, body language, and the handshakes selectively not given to us as if our Blackness might rub off. We have no choice but to internalize the fear of those that see us, then feel inclined to take action to create physical distance between them and ourselves. Many minorities have known the isolation of social distancing long before COVID-19 required it of us, though there is no disease we carry that can kill anyone other than the disease of our lack of conformity killing someone's sense of normalcy.

Our suspicion has become cemented into who we were with every story told by our parents and grandparents of rocks being hurled toward them while "Nigger, nigger, nigger!" was yelled over and over again on the school playgrounds or walking in neighborhoods with no one willing to advocate for them. Our suspicion was cemented into our psyches every time we'd go into a store to shop, like anyone else, only to be met by a sales associate following us around the store while others roamed freely without supervision. Our suspicion was cemented with every news report or article that would come out reporting yet another belief about Black people that took from our worth as humans. Our suspicion was cemented every time we'd form a friendship with a white person who we thought really accepted us for our differences, not in spite of them, but then would turn on us the moment we spoke of the history of our ancestors being stolen and then sold by the very white America that made this country what it is today. Our suspicion was cemented every time, the way we styled our braids, coils, or kinks, was deemed "Unprofessional hair" or we were challenged on our personal decision to wear a weave or a wig because our ability to choose our hair like we choose our clothes wasn't understood. Our suspicions were cemented.

There is so much that can be said about how we all got here. How this division has been able to go on for so long unchecked or how taking two steps forward and four steps back, year after year, has been deemed progress in the minds of those who benefit from regression. Really it all starts with fear. On all sides. Fear of what you aren't familiar with, fear of our history, fear of our future, fear of what if things change, fear of what if it stays the same, fear of being wrong, fear of being seen and understood, fear of understanding, fear of coming together, and fear of staying apart. If you draw a line connecting all the dots, so much of it leads us all back to fear. We have been pinned against each other by history, the media, and by those who cling to their traditions of fear and suspicion, but that doesn't have to be our way. It doesn't have to be your way.

I know it doesn't always feel safe going out on your own and paving a new way to the future. Inwardly, I know it feels like jumping from a plane with no parachute or it's like that feeling you get in your stomach when you're about to take that first steep descent on a roller coaster ride. It can feel impending because even if this isn't the first time you're required to be brave, this kind of bravery is different. This isn't cutting 12 inches of length off your hair, then leaving the salon feeling like you're ready to take on the world kind of brave. This is cutting off some inherited beliefs, shedding layers of traditions, biases, and having to possibly take on a world you don't yet totally understand - kind of brave. It's about possibly having to do it on your own depending on the heart stance of those around you. Which is why it's going to take more than courage. It's going to take conviction.

That's why I'm here. That's why this book. That's why right now. It's not some coincidence that you've made it to the last chapter. Call me nutty but I don't even believe that you are finishing this book only by the sheer will to do so. In my heart and soul, I believe you are still in this with me because you've been feeling the beautiful distraction. Sometimes it feels like the tiny hands of a child tugging at the hem of your shirt trying to get your attention, one that you notice but can ignore while you tend to something else. Other times however, it feels all encompassing, like the hyper awareness of your mortality that you feel right after being in a car accident. I believe that you're still here with me because even after the moments of possibly feeling in disagreement with, offended by, or uncomfortable with something I've said you still feel called to look in the face of racial division and say "No more".

I'm grateful for you. I may not know you, yet I'm so grateful that you exist right now, because as long as there are those like you who seek to understand, then that means there is still something that people find worth understanding. It's not the growing pains that come along with the process of understanding ourselves and those around us that should elicit fear in you. It's the remote possibility of living in a world where we as humans no longer feel the need to seek understanding that should be feared the most. So please, keep seeking. Keep challenging your comfort zone. Keep showing up even if you need to walk away for a moment to regroup. Keep reaching out for one another, or if it's the case, start reaching out for one another. The systems and ideas that created the divide in the first place don't have to be allowed to continue to create us and shape the future. We get to choose.

If you find yourself feeling lost and lacking purpose or you wonder what you were put on this earth to do, or if you haven't yet figured out what you want to be when you grow up, let me assure you that you are meant to be a powerful force in this world. You were born to be a mover of barriers, a shaker of standards, and a builder of bridges. Let me tell you right now that there is a purpose so deep and so wide standing before you that if you seek to fulfill it every day you will never run out of work to be done or ways to do it....and that purpose is love. Just. Love.

References

[1]Children's Bureau (Administration on Children, Youth and Families, Administration for Children and Families) of the U.S. Department of Health and Human Services. 2018. *Child Maltreatment 2018.* Annual, Washington D.C.: U.S Department of Health and Human Services. Accessed August 2020. https://www.acf.hhs.gov/sites/default/files/documents/cb/cm2018.pdf.

[2]Elfrink, Tim. 2020. "Morning Mix." *The Washington Post.* June 25. Accessed August 15, 2020. https://www.washingtonpost.com/nation/2020/06/25/wilmington-racist-police-recording/.

Author

Andrea Krystal is an un-apologetic late bloomer and chronic snooze button hitter, who can usually be found barefoot and curled up in a chair somewhere, drinking the now room temperature tea that she's reheated probably a dozen times already. She didn't dream of writing a book one day and she never fantasized of fame. What she did dream of, was being a part of something that would make others feel more understood. To help people feel more connected with one another and to, in many ways, help herself heal from the brokenness of her own sense of feeling misunderstood in the world. Andrea loves thrifting, motivating women to become interested in themselves again, and otherwise spends far too much money on plants. She lives in Michigan, close to the family and friends she loves, and with the plants she spends all her money on.

To reach Andrea for speaking engagements, book club discussions etc., contact her via:
Website: www.andreakrystal.com
Email: connect@andreakrystal.com
Fb: https://www.facebook.com/ItsAndreaKrystal
IG: https://www.instagram.com/ItsAndreaKrystal

CPSIA information can be obtained
at www.ICGtesting.com
Printed in the USA
BVHW041009210422
634952BV00018B/887